Managing Health Care Costs

Private Sector Innovations

Sean Sullivan
with Polly M. Ehrenhaft

American Enterprise Institute for Public Policy Research
Washington and London

Sean Sullivan is senior analyst at AEI's Center for Health Policy Studies. Polly M. Ehrenhaft is a Washington-based health policy analyst.

This volume was prepared under a grant from the J. M. Foundation of New York, for whose support we are grateful. I want to give special thanks to Richard Van Bell, director of health care at Deere and Company; Ronald Hurst, manager of health care planning at Caterpillar Tractor Company; James Mortimer, executive director of the Midwest Business Group on Health; Peter Singer, executive director of the Utah Health Cost Management Foundation; and Melinda Schwenk, who prepared the manuscripts. S.S.

Library of Congress Cataloging in Publication Data

Sullivan, Sean.
Managing health care costs.

(AEI studies ; 406)
1. Insurance, Health—United States. 2. Medical care—United States—Cost control. I. Ehrenhaft, Polly M. II. Title. III. Series.
HD7102.U4S93 1984 338.4'33621'0973 84-6390
ISBN 0-8447-3557-4
ISBN 0-8447-3556-6 (pbk.)

1 3 5 7 9 10 8 6 4 2

AEI Studies 406

Printed in the United States of America

COVER: Photograph courtesy of George Washington University Hospital.

Contents

Foreword

This volume—made possible by a grant from the J. M. Foundation of New York—carries further work that began more than two years ago, when AEI's Center for Health Policy Research surveyed private sector initiatives to contain health care costs and published *Market Reforms in Health Care*. The present volume offers case studies in greater depth, focusing on two companies and two coalitions that have been pacesetters in the cost containment effort.

The case studies exhibit a wide range of responses to rising costs by private payers. Data collection and utilization review stay within the system of health care delivery and financing that prevails in the United States and try to make it perform less expensively. Development of health maintenance organizations (HMOs) and efforts to change restrictive state laws open the health care marketplace to competitive delivery and financing systems.

The second part of the book is an edited transcript of an AEI seminar on private sector initiatives in health care, held in July 1983. It brought together a large and diverse group of panelists to discuss the development of new models of cost containment and the shifting of hospital costs from public programs to private payers, a major issue. Thanks to the J. M. Foundation, we can share the proceedings of that seminar with a much larger audience than was able to attend.

The programs conducted by AEI's Center for Health Policy Research have focused on issues in the forefront of public debate. In *A New Approach to the Economics of Health Care* (1981), edited by Mancur Olson, we reviewed experiences with health care regulation in the United States and abroad and assessed the general merit of market-oriented changes in health policy. In *Market Reforms in Health Care* (1983), edited by Jack A. Meyer, the center's director, we explored some of the key decisions to be made and the barriers to be overcome in implementing a system of incentives for cost-conscious choices in health care. And in *Restructuring Medicaid* (1983), edited by Sean Sullivan and Rosemary Gibson and also funded by the J. M. Foundation, we studied state and local initiatives to reform the delivery and financing of care under Medicaid. Now, in the present volume, we look more closely at the potential for changes in the private sector side of health care markets, which can have an important influence on public policy.

WILLIAM J. BAROODY, JR.
President
American Enterprise Institute

Introduction and Overview

Private sector initiatives to contain health care costs have become a striking feature of the changing health care marketplace in the past few years. Not long ago most private employers did little more than grumble as they paid ever-escalating premiums for their employees' health insurance. Serious efforts at cost containment by business, labor, and insurers were the scattered exceptions to a general rule of inertia. Now, in many areas of the country, action is fast replacing talk. The short case studies in this volume are good evidence of the shift that has been taking place.

The American Enterprise Institute's Center for Health Policy Research has been studying this shift for more than two years. Since our first survey of private sector initiatives, we have watched them develop to the point where they are playing a large part in changing the structure and operation of the health care system. With all the attention given the problems of the Medicare program by the press, it is easily forgotten that employers still pay the largest share of the nation's health care bill. Their actions are at least as important as reforms being made in Medicare and Medicaid toward effecting the single most important change needed in the system—giving providers and users incentives to be more conscious of costs in their provision and use of services.

The actions of companies and coalitions like those presented here are having such an effect. Utilization review based on good data is changing providers' practice patterns when payers insist on it. And health maintenance organizations (HMOs) and other alternative delivery and financing systems, such as the new preferred provider organizations (PPOs), are making the entire system more competitive.

The individual companies studied are Deere and Company and Caterpillar Tractor Company, two large, traditional mid-American manufacturing concerns that have been ahead of most private employers in curbing runaway health care costs. Although their approaches have differed, as the case studies show, Deere and Caterpillar have both done what other companies are discovering they must do to gain any control over costs—treat health care as a managerial rather than merely an administrative function. This may seem an obvious point—as most important points are—but it requires companies to go beyond the stage of complaints to find out and put into effect ways to influence the behavior of both their employees who consume medical services and the providers who supply them. This is what companies like Deere and Caterpillar were doing well ahead of most others, and the evolution of their efforts makes instructive reading.

Both companies have also actively encouraged development of alternative health plans to give their employees a choice, and many employees have chosen to join such plans. At the same time, the companies have signed contracts with existing professional standards review organizations (PSROs) to review the utilization of services by employees who remain in the traditional insurance plan.

The other two case studies examine what have loosely come to be called "business coalitions," although one of the two is a broader combination of parties that might better be termed a community coalition. The Midwest Business Group on Health (MBGH) is a regional group of more than a hundred companies that has evolved from modest beginnings into a growing force for change in a multistate area. It has concentrated on helping its members to develop basic health management tools, such as good data on utilization and costs, as well as educating company executives who serve as trustees on hospital boards. These activities do not attempt to change the system dramatically or promote more competitive kinds of health plans, such as HMOs; they focus on such steps as the redesign of the health benefit package and the careful use of comparative data on the cost patterns of health service providers to improve the performance of the existing system. Within these limits, the MBGH has developed usable models and standards for its members. It is also developing local chapters and user groups to help them deal with providers and insurers where they do business. Thus it has stressed the efficacy of basic tools and of the organization and the collective will to use them. Deere and Caterpillar are members of the MBGH.

The Utah Health Cost Management Foundation has also worked to develop better data and has undertaken a major effort to educate consumers by publishing controversial information on comparative hospital costs. But the foundation is most noteworthy for its active championing of competition in the health care marketplace.

This strong commitment to a more market-oriented competitive system has shown itself in the foundation's efforts to help get more alternative health plans and delivery systems established in the Salt Lake City area. It has done marketing and feasibility studies and analyzed referral patterns for potential sponsors of new prepaid plans. These efforts have recently paid off in the formation of such a plan by a highly respected multispecialty clinic, a move that the foundation believes will open the doors for others to follow.

The foundation has also shown itself willing to confront the medical establishment over the question of a competitive versus a regulated market. It did so by pushing for repeal of insurance laws that impede formation of preferred provider organizations. Few, if any, coalitions have been willing to tackle providers so directly.

Taken together, these four case studies speak of the diversity of private initiatives that are, nonetheless, aimed at a similar goal of containing the rise in health care costs for private payers. But this goal will not be achieved if costs continue to be "contained" in public programs by being shifted to the private sector. This makes efforts to reform Medicare and Medicaid payment systems vitally important to private employers as well.

An AEI seminar in July 1983 dealt with this issue of the cost shift and the private sector response to it—which is, increasingly, to seek a regulatory "solution" through an all-payers statute, as in Massachusetts. This solution runs counter to more competitively oriented market innovations such as preferred provider organizations, which were also discussed as new models of cost containment. The seminar brought together individuals with the widest range of perspectives that could be gathered around one table, and their discussion provides a larger backdrop for the private sector efforts described in the case studies. The private debate over all-payers rate setting is perhaps the latest expression of the continuing public policy debate over regulation versus competition in health care. It may seem ironic to find support for the regulatory approach in the corporate sector, but this support reflects the general disagreement over what to do about soaring health care costs. Nevertheless, companies and coalitions around the nation are trying to do something about their own costs and in doing so are having a major effect on the health care system and on the shaping of public policy.

Part One
Case Studies

Deere and Company

Deere's corporate efforts to manage health care costs go back to the late 1960s and early 1970s. The company's annual health care bill as recently as 1972 was $20 million. At that time it decided to self-insure and to self-administer health and accident claims of employees, dependents, and retirees. By self-administering its claims, the company built a data base on utilization and costs—information that companies were not generally getting from their insurers. Deere was one of the earliest corporations to become self-insured (a recent survey of 500 firms found that nearly 40 percent of them were now at least partially self-insured).

Having established an efficient claims payment mechanism, Deere came to realize that it nevertheless remained powerless to control the ever-rising health care bills fed into the mechanism. Self-insurance and self-administration produced only administrative cost savings, which—though nice to have—were minuscule compared with the price tag for delivery of services to its employees. By 1977 the company's health care bill had climbed to $60 million, and it decided to conduct a thorough study of how it was managing its health care costs.

The study prompted two major decisions: (1) the company should reorganize itself to give sufficient management attention to the task; (2) after putting its own house in order, it should try to act jointly with providers in dealing with health care issues.

Deere's first step was to form a new health care department that brought together various functions concerned with health care that were scattered around the company. By creating a high-level position for the manager of this department, the company made plain that it was serious about doing more than just studying the problem. This position was recently raised to a higher managerial level, indicating Deere's commitment to gaining greater control of its costs by managing rather than merely administering the health care function.

Deere also created a health care systems group to manage its claims processing and develop the claims data base needed to try to gain some control over utilization. A manager of health care services who knew the health care system was added to the staff. He began working with health systems agencies (HSAs) and professional standards review organizations (PSROs), with providers identified as high utilizers of hospital inpatient services, with Deere's own labor relations staff to change union agreements to establish inpatient precertification procedures, and with the twenty-five company executives serving on hospitals' boards of trustees to educate them about the health care system.

Deere looked carefully at the data it was collecting on utilization and found that its employees in Illinois and Iowa, where it is a major employer, were hospitalized much more than the norm for the surrounding communities; Deere employees averaged 1,300–1,400 days of hospitalization per 1,000 population, compared with averages of about 1,000 days in the communities. This discovery led the company to contract with PSROs in western Illinois and in Iowa to conduct both admission and concurrent stay review for its employees and to implement a selective preadmission certification procedure.

The company has been encouraged by the results of these actions. After three years of utilization review there were big drops in inpatient days and admissions per 1,000 and in average length of stay in both states. The declines were on the order of 21–27 percent for inpatient days, 14–15 percent for admissions, and 1/2–1 day for average length of stay.

Deere was one of the earliest companies to act on the need to collect good data and use them to review utilization patterns. Others have done so more recently, either individually or as members of business coalitions. Few companies, however, have taken Deere's active stance in promoting and developing health maintenance organizations (HMOs) as alternatives to traditional health insurance plans for its employees. The company has acted more boldly, perhaps, because its top management became committed to HMO development. It also enjoyed the advantages of being the largest employer in several of its locations and having some good data on utilization.

In 1978 the company hired consultants experienced in developing and operating both group and individual practice HMOs. It approached medical society leaders in the Quad Cities area—its corporate headquarters area of Moline, Illinois, and Davenport, Iowa—to discuss the cost escalation problem and persuaded a group of doctors to band together to form an individual practice association (IPA) model HMO. The group practice model would have permitted greater control of costs, but Deere decided on the IPA to get more doctors to join, to avoid creating excess capacity in the area, and to reduce the size of its own investment (since in an IPA the member physicians work out of their own offices). The company not only acted as catalyst in the process by working through the medical societies but provided front-end financing through a $600,000 loan and contributed management help in setting up the HMO.

The first year of operation saw 30 percent of Deere's local work force, or 12,000 employees, sign up, along with about 40 percent of the local physicians. Company enrollment is now up to 23,000 employees, dependents, and retirees, and 7,000 people not affiliated with Deere have also joined. Physicians continue to be paid on a fee-for-service basis rather than on a capitation basis as in a group practice HMO, but they are put at risk for up to 10 percent of their fees—although they have not lost any money yet. Deere has also found that hospital utilization—measured by admissions, inpatient days, and length of stay—is lower than under its regular indemnity plan. This is a common experience in HMOs and is often attributed to risk selection; that is, healthier people join HMOs. The company has found no major difference, however, in age or sex distribution between its HMOs and its traditional insurance plan.

The favorable outcome of its Quad Cities venture led Deere to work with the business and medical communities in Waterloo and Dubuque, Iowa, two other cities where it has major concentrations of employees, to establish similar HMOs there. It has enrolled 30,000 employees, dependents, and retirees at Waterloo and another 6,500 at Dubuque. Companywide, 40 percent of those eligible have chosen an HMO.

The company indicates that, with the drop in hospital utilization both by those enrolled in HMOs and through the PSRO program for those in the traditional indemnity plan, the rate of increase in health care costs has been slowed. Deere's newly implemented on-line claims processing system allows it to compare data from the HMOs with data from the PSROs that perform utilization review for those still enrolled in the company insurance plan. The company also notes that the United Auto Workers and other unions with which it has collective bargaining agreements have supported the development of HMOs and are represented on their boards of trustees. As the largest private employer in Iowa, Deere may be changing the health care market as well; Blue Cross is reported to be considering a plan for a statewide HMO network.

The last part of Deere's health management strategy is what the company refers to as its involvement and awareness program. This program includes some activities that have already been mentioned, such as serving on the boards of HSAs where they still exist and running a hospital trustee education program for its own executives. The company is also active in coalitions that are working collaboratively on health care cost containment. It is an active member of the Midwest Business Group on Health, a regional coalition that has emphasized data collection and utilization review; Deere's manager of health care services served for two years as its chairman. (The activities of the Midwest Business Group on Health are described elsewhere in this report.)

A good example of the kind of results that can be obtained from active coalition efforts is the recent establishment by the Iowa General Assembly of a state Health Data Commission to collect and disseminate data from providers, the state Medicaid program, and third-party payers. As a member of the Iowa Business-Labor Coalition, Deere worked through the Health Policy Corporation of Iowa (HPCI)—which replaced the local HSA—to help get the bill passed. The HPCI's board of trustees represents all the major private parties concerned about health care costs in the state—employers, unions, physicians, hospitals, and insurers. Their interest coincided with the state's concern at the rising cost of public programs, and the result was the first legislatively mandated data-reporting system in the nation. The HPCI has applied for a grant from the Robert Wood Johnson Foundation under a program to demonstrate the efficacy of community-based coalitions. Deere's corporate philosophy favors this kind of cooperative effort over a more adversarial approach to dealing with providers.

The director of health care attributes whatever progress the company has made to an approach that emphasizes three basic things: (1) developing good data on utilization and costs; (2) working with providers to put those data to use in reducing unnecessary utilization; and (3) having the support of top management. Deere believes that the health care system can be changed by these kinds of efforts at the local level. The company favors voluntary behavioral change by the health care providers in the system, rather than change mandated by government in such forms as rate regulation. But it admits that a dramatic reduction in hospital utilization by its employees has so far failed—for whatever reasons—to produce a similar reduction in costs. Deere's total bill for health benefits has continued to climb, reaching $100 million in 1983.

Caterpillar Tractor Company

Caterpillar Tractor Company's health care bill for its U.S. employees was about $35 million in 1973, reached nearly $100 million five years later, and exceeded $155 million in 1982. The company's health care costs have more than doubled since 1976 and now total nearly $2,500 per employee, or almost 10 percent of payroll costs. This rapid escalation has led Caterpillar to undertake cost containment efforts both inside and outside the company.

Caterpillar began administering its own claims in the early 1950s. By doing so, it has accumulated a broad data base that it uses for cost analysis. In 1978 the company contracted with the professional standards review organization (PSRO) in Peoria, where about half its domestic employees are located, to monitor hospital admissions and lengths of stay. After a year the average length of stay was reduced by one day, and admissions also declined. This favorable experience led Caterpillar to sign contracts with PSROs in other locations where it has large concentrations of employees. It now has six such contracts, and 80 percent of its hospital admissions are being reviewed. Since this review began, patient-days per 1,000 covered have been reduced by more than 300.

Benefit redesign is another avenue the company has taken in its efforts to control costs. Of course, its ability to change the health benefit plan is limited by its contract with the United Auto Workers; that is, changes must be agreed to by the union before they can be implemented. Two such changes that were negotiated in 1983 are a program of voluntary second opinions for elective surgery and a program to encourage the use of generic drugs.

The company has also added home nursing care to its plan as a newly covered benefit, integrating it into the hospital discharge system with the expectation that it will save money and in many cases be more humane than continued hospitalization. The plan also contains significant outpatient coverage for laboratory and X-ray services, ambulatory surgery, and preadmission testing. These benefits try to come to grips with the largest part of the problem of escalating health care costs—hospital costs, which have been increasing more rapidly than other medical costs.

Internal communication to and education of employees and management constitute another important part of the company's cost management strategy. Employees are regularly informed about health care costs and reminded of the potential cost-saving features of the health plan. The company also communicates regularly with its executives who serve as trustees on local hospital boards about the health care system and hospital costs.

Caterpillar has considered ways to encourage its employees to develop healthier life styles, recognizing that staying healthy is ultimately the most effective way to control health care costs. Lacking evidence of the effectiveness of formal programs to change employees' behavior, it has not instituted a corporate wellness or preventive health program, although it has had an in-house alcoholism program for ten years and has held smoking cessation and hypertension clinics at various plants.

A former Peoria physician was appointed medical director of group insurance in 1981. His responsibilities include monitoring claims that exceed usual and customary fees, reviewing claims and data for overutilization of outpatient procedures, helping to train claims processors, and assisting in claims audits.

Caterpillar's group insurance manager works with "third-party committees" of physicians, dentists, and pharmacists to resolve specific complaints in those benefit areas. This manager recently received a Pew Foundation fellowship for study at Boston University's Center for Health Studies. The company uses third-party committees and specialty society contacts extensively to educate physicians and dentists about the costs of abuse, overutilization, or lack of knowledge of costs on their part. The professional societies have been supportive of the company's efforts to control abuse; for example, local medical societies have helped prepare guidelines for physicians on billing practices for laboratory fees and components of surgical fees.

The company has involved itself with several outside efforts to contain health care costs. Several of its managers serve on the boards of local health systems agencies, with the aim of getting a better grip on the existing health care system. The company believes that corporate involvement in the process can improve it. This involvement, in the view of Caterpillar and many other companies, should be chiefly at the local community level, where decisions can be reached by working with the other participants in the system and on the basis of firsthand knowledge. Where appropriate, the company has encouraged organizations that it supports with contributions of money or manpower—including local chambers of commerce as well as state and national groups—to become involved in the control of health care costs.

Spurred by rapidly growing hospital costs in Illinois—the second highest per capita in the nation, after Massachusetts—Caterpillar has moved to offer health maintenance organizations (HMOs) to more of its employees as alternatives to its traditional health insurance plan. The company has contributed management help and seed money for feasibility studies and, where study findings have been encouraging, for development. Feasibility studies in York, Pennsylvania (where Caterpillar's local benefits manager served on the board of the steering committee), and in Decatur, Illinois, two years ago concluded that the local health care markets were not ready to sustain HMOs, and it was decided not to go ahead. Blue Cross has since started its own HMO in York, indicating that the market may be changing there, as it is in many other cities. And Maxicare is examining the Decatur market.

Caterpillar now offers an HMO option to its employees in a growing number of cities, and more employees are choosing HMOs. The company makes twenty HMOs available at its various locations and has enrolled more than 7,000 employees in them—of an active U.S. work force of 43,000. The highest percentage enrolled is, not surprisingly, in California, where 50 percent of Caterpillar workers at San Diego and San Leandro are in well-established plans.

Already 1,657 Caterpillar employees in Peoria are enrolled in Maxicare/Intergroup, a ten-year-old HMO that Caterpillar contributed capital and managerial time to help start. Healthplan of Central Illinois, an individual practice association (IPA) HMO, has already signed up 1,104 nonhourly workers and will soon be offered to hourly employees as well. Some 13 percent of active employees and 5 percent of retirees in Peoria are in these two plans. And the Peoria example is being followed elsewhere—for example, in efforts to offer new HMOs in Decatur and Joliet, Illinois, and Lafayette, Indiana.

The company shows an active concern for making HMOs work, rather than just offering them to its employees without regard for their satisfaction with the quality of services received. Caterpillar's manager of health care planning served on an employer advisory group for the Maxicare/Intergroup HMO, which is headquartered in Chicago and has enrolled 550 Caterpillar employees in Aurora, Illinois. And he has been on the boards of the National Association of Employers on HMOs and of the National Industry Council for HMO Development. Caterpillar's employee relations manager in Davenport, Iowa, is on the board of the Quad City Health Plan, an HMO of the IPA type started by Deere, where 1,275 Caterpillar employees and retirees are enrolled.

Caterpillar also works through a dozen state and local coalitions trying to contain health care costs. In 1978 it helped start a Peoria business coalition, since combined with the area's health systems agency, which includes representatives of providers and of labor as well. The coalition has encouraged employers to offer HMOs, with considerable success; thirty area companies now offer them, up from only four in 1978. Labor's support has been important in this effort; for example, the United Auto Workers' local has worked with Caterpillar and other employers to encourage its members to enroll in HMOs. The coalition has successfully encouraged fourteen other companies since 1978 to join Caterpillar in using the PSRO for utilization review. Caterpillar's manager of health care planning is a director of the U.S. Chamber of Commerce Clearinghouse for Coalitions and a past member of the American Hospital Association Advisory Council on Coalitions.

Caterpillar has also shown interest in the cost-saving potential of the newly emerging preferred provider organizations (PPOs). As a self-insured company, it could negotiate directly with physicians and hospitals for discounted fee schedules. It intends to support legislative initiatives in Illinois and other states to follow California's example in removing legal and regulatory impediments to the establishment of PPOs. It has no PPO contracts at present, however, and is concerned about the effect on high-cost public aid and teaching hospitals if it contracts with lower-cost hospitals where its employees are concentrated.

In 1983 Caterpillar joined with other Peoria employers and three major hospitals to form the Peoria Area Hospital Council. Its purpose is to increase cooperation and reduce unnecessary duplication of services, and the hospitals have agreed to share new technology.

Like many other private payers in the health care system, Caterpillar is increasingly concerned about the "cost shift"—the failure of public programs like Medicare and Medicaid to reimburse hospitals for the full cost of providing care and the consequent shifting of the uncompensated costs to private payers like Caterpillar. The size of this shift has been estimated at about $8 billion nationally in 1983 and $450 million in Illinois alone. Because of recent changes in Medicare and Medicaid reimbursement rules, it is expected to grow much larger in the next few years as even more costs are shifted. Caterpillar estimates that about $12 million of its $76.6 million hospital bill in 1982—or nearly one-sixth—resulted from cost shifting. The pressure to shift more Medicaid costs to private payers is likely to grow in Illinois because of the state's budget squeeze and the continuing rise in hospital capital expenditures.

Like many companies, Caterpillar is frustrated by an inability to slow the rise of hospital charges despite considerable effort. Such frustration has led the Illinois Health Care Coalition—which includes Caterpillar and other employers as well as representatives of organized labor among its members—to sponsor a legislative attempt to establish a prospective cap for hospital revenues and mitigate further shifting of costs from public to private payers. The proposal—Senate Bill 495—would create an all-payers scheme similar to that enacted in 1982 in Massachusetts. Under an all-payers system, both public and private payers must reimburse hospitals for a fixed percentage of their charges, with the percentages fixed by the state (this system requires a federal waiver of customary Medicare reimbursement rules). Senate Bill 495 would establish an Illinois Hospital Revenue Commission to set allowable hospital revenue limits for each category of payer in the interim while developing a long-term solution.

Employers were the driving force behind the recent enactment of such a measure in Massachusetts, as they are behind the effort in Illinois—although not all employers support the proposal. Caterpillar feels it is a necessary but temporary measure until the health care market can be made to function more effectively. Caterpillar's manager of health care planning serves on a technical advisory panel appointed by the state senate to suggest amendments to Senate Bill 495. The Illinois Hospital Association has introduced its own legislative cap alternative to the bill, and concern about the need for a statewide approach to hospital cost control has been heightened in a state where providers' groups hold considerable political power.

Midwest Business Group on Health

The Midwest Business Group on Health (MBGH) is a coalition of 120 companies in eight midwestern states that is concerned about slowing the rate of increase in health care costs. Although a number of business coalitions have been formed to influence the costs of health care services in a single state or urban area, the MBGH is the only organization serving an entire region. Its staff serves as a technical resource for member companies throughout the region. Its agenda is a careful blend of policy development and research and technical assistance for local action-oriented projects.

In 1979 the Washington Business Group on Health did a feasibility study on whether to open a Chicago office. Instead, the companies headquartered in the area decided to start an independent organization. The MBGH began in February 1980 with only 15 charter members and grew steadily to its current 120 member companies, which provide health benefits to over 3 million people. These employees and their dependents make up more than 5 percent of the population in Illinois, Indiana, Iowa, Michigan, Minnesota, Missouri, Ohio, and Wisconsin.

Members are both single- and multiple-site companies and include many of the large corporations operating in the Midwest. Both Deere and Company and Caterpillar Tractor Company, whose activities in health care cost management are described elsewhere in this report, are members of the coalition. The MBGH encourages the development of local chapters that can coordinate projects among area members. Specific projects are usually initiated either by individual members or by the local chapters. Thus far there are chapters in Chicago, Minneapolis/St. Paul, and Rockford, Illinois.

The primary thrust of the MBGH is to motivate and assist corporations to develop and implement health cost management tools. It emphasizes those projects that will have the greatest potential payoff for its members. The four project areas in which it has been most active are utilization review, data management, education of trustees, and design of benefit plans.

Utilization review programs are targeted for further development because MBGH members with operational programs report returns on their investments ranging from 3 to 1 to 12 to 1. The purpose of the programs is to evaluate the necessity of hospital admissions and lengths of stay for member companies' employees. The MBGH staff helps members initiate and maintain effective utilization review programs primarily through technical assistance. As an indication of the emphasis given this effort, the coalition has already published two editions of its business guide for establishing successful utilization review programs. The MBGH has helped to develop programs that are now operating in Rockford and Springfield, Illinois, Minneapolis/St. Paul, Cedar Rapids, Iowa, and Battle Creek, Michigan. More than one-third of MBGH member companies have contracts for continuing utilization review programs.

A noteworthy areawide effort is under way in Chicago. The Chicago area chapter has joined forces with local hospitals, physicians, and insurers to form a new cooperative organization to operate a utilization review program. Incorporated in December 1982, the Chicago Health Economics Council (CHEC) has spent two years developing a private concurrent utilization review program for Cook County, Illinois. CHEC will be the primary contractor for participating corporations, insurers, and hospitals. It will develop policies and performance standards, manage finances, and report results to participants. The local professional review organization, Health Review Systems, Inc., of Chicago, will perform the concurrent utilization review and analyze and distribute data reports. Information about the program has been disseminated to corporations in the Chicago area, and as soon as a sufficient number of companies and insurers have agreed to participate, operations will begin.

Data are fundamental for identifying areas of excess expenditures for health benefits, for finding problems in health service utilization or price, and for monitoring the results of cost management initiatives. The MBGH has focused on developing standards and models for data collection. A model format for the presentation of claims data has been developed, for example, and several of the major insurance companies and Blue Cross plans have adopted it for providing data to their MBGH customers. Most recently an MBGH committee completed work on specifications for a minimum set of data elements for claims processing. Uniform data sets will support improved management reporting and enable comparisons of companies to be made.

"User groups," in which member companies work in groups with individual insurance carriers, are the MBGH's most popular program. Currently, three-fifths of all members are organized into ten groups to share and use claims data. User groups meet regularly to analyze patterns of health service use and costs. The pooled data reports form the basis for cost management programs within individual companies. Depending on circumstances, employers might pursue external strategies, such as negotiating with or educating hospitals, physicians, or hospital trustees, or internal strategies, such as changing benefit plans or creating employee education programs.

The user group in Minnesota is attempting to get data beyond those supplied by the participating carrier. To get a more complete understanding of employees' use of health services, member companies have requested comparable data from area HMOs. The HMOs' experience with employees can then be compared with the experience shown by insurers.

A third major target area for the MBGH is education of trustees. Because the majority of hospital trustees are established leaders in business, increasing their understanding and effectiveness provides an excellent opportunity to shape hospital policies. Responding to members' interest, the MBGH designed a program to educate business leaders who are trustees. It provides pertinent information in areas that relate to cost management, such as hospital finance, productivity, and long-range planning. The program also serves as a forum for communicating and planning with hospitals and insurers.

A final programmatic area for the MBGH is design of employee benefit plans. In 1983 the MBGH surveyed all its members about the changes they were making in their health benefit programs. The purpose of the survey was to capitalize on innovations that might already have been introduced by members. As a follow-up activity, a task force is being formed to consider models for benefit plans.

A corollary to benefit design is employee education. Informed consumers use the health care system more cost-efficiently. Moreover, corporations risk severe public relations consequences if employees are not properly informed of changes in their health benefits. For these reasons, the MBGH has written a paper on managing health benefit costs and educating employees on using the health care system. Periodic conferences and seminars are also held to inform member companies about management techniques for educating consumers.

A major benefit for all MBGH member companies is the opportunity to participate with other businesses, providers, and insurers in conferences and workshops that offer concrete, usable information on health management tools. The MBGH also holds an annual meeting and publishes a quarterly newsletter for its members. Merely by joining together in an organized group, corporations increase the collective voice of business in the community. When providers recognize business as a participating partner in the health care system, they are more responsive to the needs of employers.

The Midwest Business Group on Health has chosen not to strive for goals that it believes are remote from its central mission. Thus it has not lobbied for political or legislative changes, nor has it actively promoted the development of such alternative reimbursement systems as HMOs or PPOs. Instead, it has focused on activities in health care that are within its direct sphere of influence. The MBGH encourages individual members to be activists and provides all the technical assistance its small staff can muster. The recent introduction into the Medicare program of fixed payments based on diagnostic-related groups (DRGs) for hospitals may shift the activities of the coalition somewhat from a project orientation toward advocacy. The private sector can respond to the new cost-cutting system introduced by government into public health care programs by demanding that the DRG system also be used for private payers. Employers can exercise such influence with providers by working collectively.

The latest project of the MBGH is an advisory panel that is charged with selecting an appropriate primary payment system to control companies' costs while ensuring no decline in the quality of care. The panel is drawn from business and labor, the academic community, the insurance industry, and providers. It is supervising the design and implementation of payment system reforms that member companies will experiment with on a pilot basis beginning in the second half of 1984.

Utah Health Cost Management Foundation

Health care costs in Utah are below the national average by numerous measures. Hospital expenditures per capita and per admission are 20–25 percent lower, partly because of much lower utilization, that is, fewer admissions and shorter lengths of stay. Nevertheless, the trend of health care costs in Utah is similar to that in the rest of the nation, with per capita hospital expenditures growing faster than the national average. The rapid rise of costs has helped to drive the state's Medicaid budget up at an average rate of more than 20 percent a year since 1976, while employers have been absorbing 15–30 percent annual increases in health insurance premiums.

This situation concerned community leaders who wanted to keep the state's budget balanced and keep employment costs down to attract new business. Many states in similar straits have enacted rate review statutes to regulate hospital prices, thus moving the health care system toward a public utility model. Utah has not historically favored government regulation in most sectors of the economy; so in 1978 the legislature commissioned a study to determine the extent of health care cost increases in the state and to recommend remedial actions. The final report—by Lewin and Associates—recommended passage of a certificate-of-need statute as an interim measure to contain costs and avoid the loss of federal funds; more important, the report urged formation of a private group to act as a catalyst for a market-oriented approach to containing costs in the longer run. In 1980 the Utah Health Cost Management Foundation (UHCMF) was formed to play this role.

The UHCMF is a coalition of major employers, employee groups, insurers, and providers. It was established with a grant from the John A. Hartford Foundation to stimulate market forces to make the health care system more competitive. Its board of directors reflects the broad array of interests that have been gathered into one organization; there are representatives of the Utah State Medical Association, the Salt

Lake County Medical Society, the Mormon church, the University of Utah Medical Center, the state AFL-CIO, the state Department of Health, Blue Cross/Blue Shield, the Family Health Plan—the only big health maintenance organization (HMO) in the Salt Lake City area—a large private hospital and health services corporation, the state small business corporation, several private insurance companies, and several of the state's major corporate employers, such as Kennecott. The foundation is not just a business coalition but a community coalition of many parties interested in containing health care costs through private actions rather than government edicts.

During its first two years the UHCMF chose four major tasks on which to concentrate: (1) improving the design of employee health insurance plans; (2) improving the administration of those plans; (3) educating the community about the health care system; and (4) promoting competitive alternative delivery systems and preferred provider organizations (PPOs). The first three tasks are generally uncontroversial and similar to what many other coalitions are doing. They are largely short-term efforts to encourage more cost-effective utilization of the health care system, in part by making both consumers and providers more aware of the costs of their actions. The fourth task, however—promoting development of alternative delivery systems—requires at least several years before any results may be apparent and is more controversial. It challenges the dominance of the traditional fee-for-service medical establishment directly rather than merely trying to influence it. Nevertheless, the foundation has pressed ahead because of a conviction on the part of most participants that this approach is the only one that has the potential to affect costs significantly by changing the incentives for providers.

Having chosen its tasks, the UHCMF developed a strategy for implementing the market approach, including specific actions to be carried out in its third year. The strategy has six parts, or six sets of actions to be taken: (1) developing community support for the market approach; (2) encouraging short-term cost control initiatives; (3) monitoring the performance of the health care system; (4) promoting development of competitive alternative delivery systems; (5) improving the environment for competition at the federal level; and (6) encouraging the state of Utah to promote competition in its own roles as purchaser and regulator of health care.

The first actions have been aimed at increasing awareness of the problem on the part of purchasers and providers and gaining their commitment to the market approach to dealing with it. Because a market approach involves getting various parties to act together of their own volition, it cannot succeed without a common understanding and resolve. To promote these, the UHCMF has arranged for speakers to address influential civic groups. It has sponsored meetings at which its board members from business, labor, government, or providers have acted as hosts and its own staff or nationally known figures have explained the market approach to other business, labor, and government leaders and to other providers. And it has approached important business, labor, and government leaders individually.

Through a variety of actions the UHCMF is encouraging employers to take steps to contain costs until alternative delivery systems can be more fully developed. It is evaluating major employers' benefit packages and recommending design changes to make employees more sensitive to the cost of health care. It is encouraging and, where feasible, helping the Utah Peer Review Organization (PRO) to contract with benefit administrators, health insurers, and employers to administer prior authorization and second opinion programs designed to avoid unnecessary hospitalization and surgery. It is working with third-party claims data to develop an information base that will help in administering such prior authorization programs. And it is continuing to market its consumer information pamphlets on how to use the health care system cost effectively.

No organization in Utah is responsible for gathering and analyzing data on costs or utilization for private patients (the PRO does it for Medicare and Medicaid patients). Because such information is essential to measuring the effects of any change, the UHCMF has taken several actions to monitor the health care system. These include updating and publishing periodic information on trends in costs and utilization, analyzing the data to identify the causes of cost increases, updating and expanding data on comparative hospital charges for surgical procedures, and gathering and publishing information on variations in practice patterns.

The heart of the foundation's market strategy is promoting competition by the development of alternative delivery systems. For this strategy to work, two conditions must be met: (1) there must be a diversity of strong plans to choose from; and (2) consumers must be able to make choices. The UHCMF wants to develop only plans that promise to promote competition by offering effective choices; it is not interested in plans with overlapping providers or monopolistic market power. Its actions to achieve the first condition include working with employers to encourage formation of alternative delivery systems by providers, helping interested providers by persuading them that forming alternative delivery systems is in their best financial interests, analyzing the referral patterns of existing group practices, performing market feasibility studies, and finding consultants and managers to help interested providers develop strong plans. And the UHCMF has worked with the Utah legislature to change restrictive state laws that prevent development of preferred provider plans by insurers or formation of single-service HMOs (these efforts have, so far, not succeeded). The foundation is also analyzing third-party claims data to help identify cost-effective providers and practice patterns.

To achieve the second condition, it is explaining the benefits of competition to employers, encouraging them to offer their employees a choice of plans and to make equal dollar contributions to each plan, and helping employers make accurate and understandable comparisons of benefits and premiums for employees.

The UHCMF believes that the market approach it seeks to promote is obstructed by certain federal laws and policies. Part of its action plan, consequently, calls for supporting market-oriented reforms in federal policy, such as tax-free rebates for employees who choose less costly health insurance plans with more individual cost sharing and—as a last resort—mandatory multiple choice of plans for employees. The foundation also seeks amendment of the federal HMO act to remove the requirements for community rating and open enrollment and to narrow the scope of required benefits; these actions would potentially open the marketplace to greater competition among HMOs.

The state of Utah is a large purchaser of health care for its employees as well as for Medicaid recipients and, through its own actions, can help to advance the market approach. To encourage it to do so, the UHCMF assists the Governor's Task Force on State Employee Health Benefits and urges that state employees be offered a choice of multiple health plans. It has helped the state develop and adopt a formal policy of containing costs through price competition and market forces. The foundation has encouraged the Division of Health Care Financing to obtain waivers that allow it to make greater use of alternative delivery systems for Medicaid enrollees (the state has obtained such waivers and is implementing a case management system for Medicaid recipients as well as continuing to enroll them in the Family Health Plan HMO). And it has sought deregulation of the health care system where that can help competition to develop.

The UHCMF has compiled a lengthy list of actions that it believes will further its strategy for promoting the market approach, and it is pursuing many of them. It must now get new funding if it is to continue, since this is the final year of its grant from the Hartford Foundation.

The relatively small size of most Utah employers and the state's still relatively low health care costs have made it more difficult to gain a strong commitment to the coalition's efforts. Nevertheless, the UHCMF is pressing ahead with its program on several major fronts. Two years ago it began a project with some of the state's largest third-party payers—Blue Cross/Blue Shield, the Department of Health, and the Deseret Mutual Benefit Association—to collect data on costs and utilization. The aim of the project was to identify individual physicians' prices and practice styles. Although a lot of information was collected, it was not of good quality. Insurers are starting to improve their data, in part because the foundation is encouraging employers to urge them to do so and in part because they are coming to see the value of a combined data base. The project resulted in publication of comparative prices for various procedures at different hospitals, with the purpose of alerting employers to the lack of competition in the system. The physician members of the board opposed publishing the prices, but they were outvoted. This information has since been updated and published for a second year.

An effort to distribute pamphlets to educate consumers about using the health care system has not gone as well as hoped because employers do not understand the need for such information. They have not yet been willing to invest the money necessary to provide this education to their employees, but the UHCMF is continuing the effort.

Utah's Professional Standards Review Organization (PSRO) was formed even before PSROs were required by the federal legislation that established Medicare and Medicaid. It is now offering second opinion and prior authorization programs to private parties. Recently a private organization called the Medical Review Institute of America has developed a second opinion program that it has begun to offer to private payers. The UHCMF has encouraged the development of such programs in the past but has found employers wary of antagonizing their employees or the physicians, who have resisted the idea. If the PSRO program fails to catch on, the foundation is prepared to offer its own second opinion program, having won approval from its board to develop one. It may still prove difficult to make it a success, however, because of physicians' resistance.

The UHCMF's relations with the medical community recently soured a bit because of its support for legislation that would open up the market for PPOs. Specifically, it has backed a bill introduced in the state senate to repeal Utah's antidiscrimination law, which prevents insurers from limiting beneficiaries' free choice of provider. The bill—Senate Bill 99—became a heated issue in the last session of the legislature, where it was defeated by strong opposition from physicians and other practitioners (although hospitals supported it). Its backers will probably try again in the next session. Half of the larger employers can already negotiate preferred provider arrangements if they wish because they are self-insured and so not subject to state insurance regulations. But, as noted earlier, they generally lack sufficient data on utilization and costs to identify efficient providers. The UHCMF is trying to remedy this situation by pushing employers to collect better data themselves or to insist on getting them from their insurers. One major insurer in the state has so far refused to participate in the data collection effort; because of its large share of the market, the claims data base is less valuable than it might otherwise be.

One UHCMF member—the Deseret Mutual Benefit Association—has developed a PPO as part of its own HMO. Deseret started the HMO as a primary care network two years ago with 400 primary care physicians; it has since reduced that number by nearly a hundred by dropping those with few patients or with high-cost profiles. The newly established PPO is a panel of specialists who have been identified as providing lower-cost care. The primary care physicians now refer all specialty care to this panel, which numbers more than 100. Deseret has enrolled 31,000 of its members—80 percent of its total membership—in the HMO.

The private employer members of the UHCMF board are united in their view of the organization's highest priority—to develop a competitive market for health care as an alternative to a regulated one. Efforts to promote competition have focused on getting new alternative delivery systems started. The Family Health Plan has been the only HMO available to the general public (Deseret Mutual's HMO serves the Mormon church). The UHCMF worked with the Salt Lake Clinic, a prestigious, multispecialty group of sixty physicians, for more than a year trying to get it to start another HMO. The foundation put together a planning document to convince the clinic that its own long-term best interests would be served by such an action, because of the increasing supply of physicians in the state and the growth of other alternative delivery systems. It analyzed the clinic's referral patterns to show where its referrals were coming from. And it did a marketing study for national HMO organizations and served as a broker between the clinic and these potential sponsors. The payoff from all this effort is the clinic's recent decision to go ahead with an HMO. The Salt Lake Clinic has joined with two other multispecialty group practice clinics to sign an HMO contract with Maxicare, and marketing began in January 1984. The UHCMF believed that if this prestigious clinic developed a plan, it would lead others to do the same and thereby open the market to effective competition, and this seems to be happening. Several other plans are now developing; for example, thirty-five independent family practitioners have signed an HMO contract with Health America.

The Utah Health Cost Management Foundation stands apart from most of the other private coalitions that have been formed to contain health care costs. Although many of them have set about collecting and improving data on utilization and costs and advising their members how to redesign health benefit plans, few if any have pushed legislative reforms that would increase competition or have worked actively to develop new alternative delivery systems (although individual companies such as Deere and Caterpillar have helped to start HMOs in cities where they are major employers; those efforts are discussed elsewhere in this report). The UHCMF's market reform strategy and activist approach make it unique. It has been willing to clash directly with providers on issues that it considers important—such as Senate Bill 99—but it has also sought their support for changes in the structure of the health care market. Despite being a community coalition of broader interests than the business only groups, it has acted more boldly than any of them to bring about change.

Part Two

Private Sector Initiatives in Health Care

Participants

Richard J. Arnould
College of Commerce and Business Administration
University of Illinois

Michael Bromberg
Federation of American Hospitals

R. E. Dedmon, M.D.
Health Services Center
Kimberly-Clark Corporation

Marvin Esch
American Enterprise Institute

Rosemary Gibson
American Enterprise Institute

Paul Ginsburg
Congressional Budget Office

Willis B. Goldbeck
Washington Business Group on Health

Glenn Hackbarth
U.S. Department of Health and Human Services

Ronald E. Henderson, M.D.
Council on Medical Service
American Medical Association

Stanley B. Jones
Health Policy Alternatives, Incorporated

Ronald P. Kaufman, M.D.
George Washington University Medical Center

David Klein
Blue Cross and Blue Shield Association

Lawrence Lewin
Lewin & Associates

Jack A. Meyer
American Enterprise Institute

Robert E. Patricelli
CIGNA Corporation

William L. Roper
Office of Policy Development
The White House

Lindon Saline
General Electric Company

Cathy Schoen
Service Employees International Union

Peter F. Singer
Utah Health Cost Management Foundation

Sean Sullivan
American Enterprise Institute

Bernard R. Tresnowski
Blue Cross and Blue Shield Association

Richard Wardrop
Alcoa Corporation

Roger Wheeler
Control Data Corporation

Robert G. Wilson, M.D.
Utah State Medical Association

This conference, held by the American Enterprise Institute for Public Policy Research in Washington, D.C., on July 19, 1983, was one in a series of programs sponsored under a grant from the Pew Memorial Trust.

New Models of Cost Containment in the Private Sector

MARVIN ESCH, American Enterprise Institute: On behalf of Bill Baroody, I extend greetings to each of you. AEI is an independent, nonprofit, nonpartisan public policy research organization, which receives grants from foundations, individuals, and corporations to do its research. We believe very strongly in the competition of ideas and that by bringing together people of differing views who have responsibilities for developing public policy, we can make a significant difference to the future of our country.

In 1974 AEI established the Center for Health Policy Research to coordinate studies and activities in the broad area of health policy. Under the able leadership of Jack Meyer, this program is now focusing on the question of the containment of health care costs, which Dr. Meyer has described as "the next social security time bomb of our public policy discussion." Today we have representatives of the providers, the insurers, and the users of health care, which will give us an opportunity to focus on the issues and on the directions we might take to provide adequate health care for all our citizens while recognizing that our resources are limited.

JACK A. MEYER, American Enterprise Institute: I, too, welcome you to the fourth in a series of seminars launched in January by our Center for Health Policy Research. The seminars are conducted under a grant from the Pew Memorial Trust, and we are very appreciative of their support of our seminars and research.

An earlier series, on the subject of market-oriented or incentives-based reforms in federal health policy, culminated in a book published earlier this year—an analysis of such proposals in federal health care policy, including major arguments in support, criticisms, and practical problems of implementation of these kinds of approaches. This current series, which runs through May 1984, focuses on local innovations in health care delivery and finance, in both the public and the private sectors. The first few seminars have dealt with reforms in Medicaid—experiments, demonstrations, waivers, and what states and local governments are doing in the way of cost management techniques that change the incentives in the system and the behavior of providers and consumers.

Today we are evaluating private sector initiatives in health care. We define the private sector broadly to include for-profit firms, non-profit groups, providers, insurers, business, and labor. Our purpose today is twofold. First, we want to share ideas and assess new models of health care cost management in the interests of refining those models and disseminating ideas so that others know what we are doing. Second, we hope to illustrate how the health care policies of the private sector are affected by government policy, to build a bridge between two sets of activities that are usually discussed separately.

When I first got involved in a major way in this field in the late 1970s, the health care dialogue was dominated by a debate between those who favored comprehensive national health insurance and those who favored equally comprehensive market-oriented approaches. I liken this debate in the ensuing years to the *Rocky I, II,* and *III* movies, in which at the end of the fight both fighters are sprawled on the mat, each having knocked the other out. Today complicated, Washington-directed grand national designs of a market or regulatory model are increasingly being questioned and put aside. That is not to say that they will not some day emerge as the way we do our business, but for a variety of reasons people have been unwilling to jump at them, and each side has knocked the other out. The market side has come up with a thousand reasons why national health insurance will not work, and those who are skeptical of a market approach have come up with a thousand reasons why that might cause trouble. While both sides make valid criticisms, the bill keeps rising.

More and more we are attacking this problem incrementally, regionally, pluralistically, and beginning to do piece by piece the kind of revision in thinking that we are unwilling to do in a grand national design. That may be more suited to the reform that is needed. Because there are huge wealth transfers at stake, to do this all at once may not be the best way to accomplish it. At the same time, federal policy has changed, but again one step at a time, and there is an honest and needed debate about whether we take steps in one direction or another. That is to say, we have to have one model, one goal, in mind; I see us moving in that direction, and I have tried to move our program of research and seminars in the direction of capturing the varied local innovations.

When we started, Medicaid was a very rigid program, carried out in much the same way throughout the country, although covered services differed. We now see different models of cost management being experimented with in the states, some moving toward all-payer systems, some toward primary care networks, lock-ins, case management approaches, rate-setting, and some toward all of the above. State and local governments are in a desperate financial position because of the cost sharing that has been sent their way. A lot of cost shifting is going on, not only down the government chain from federal to state and local but also across the country from government as a whole to the private sector.

One of our purposes today is to assess the implications for the private sector of public sector developments and vice versa. Another is to hear from a panel of experts about the kinds of things the health care industry and employers are doing to wrestle with the effects of those developments and to establish effective cost containment policies. Just as we are observing an opening up of the Medicaid program through regulatory reform and waivers to do things that would have been illegal a few years ago, so are we witnessing a more experimental attitude on the part of the private sector, a willingness to try things that a couple of years ago would have been too controversial, a dialogue between business and labor—a dialogue that often brings in the providers—and in many areas more than a dialogue, a redesign of benefits and a pluralistic approach.

I still think we need federal reform, less grandiose than some may have thought before, but we have some tough choices facing us in public programs. I now turn the seminar over to Sean Sullivan, a senior analyst at AEI.

SEAN SULLIVAN, American Enterprise Institute: When I came to AEI and the Center for Health Policy Research, the first thing I worked on was private sector initiatives in health care—a survey of what employers were doing. We wrote a paper on this subject, presented it at our Public Policy Week last December, and have since published it as one of the chapters of *Market Reforms in Health Care*. So we have had an ongoing interest in this subject, which we are continuing to pursue under a grant from the J. M. Foundation to study private sector initiatives.

We are going beyond our earlier survey and doing case studies of approaches of coalitions and individual employers to containment of health care costs. The approaches fall into two basic categories: those that attempt to change the behavior of employees and patients within the system without trying to change the structure of incentives and those that attempt to change those incentives as a somewhat more radical way of changing the behavior of the actors, the providers as well as the employees and patients. This morning we will consider both kinds of activities.

We are fortunate to have with us to introduce this morning's session and present some background on what is going on, especially among employers, Dick Wardrop, of the Alcoa Corporation. Dick has been a friend of AEI's work on health policy for some time, has participated in AEI seminars, and has been an active leader in the Washington Business Group on Health.

RICHARD WARDROP, Alcoa Corporation: Before we talk about the present, I will take a few minutes to review what has happened in the last few years; it will help us see what the private sector has been through and whether there is any indication that it may be on the brink of breaking through to something meaningful. My brief history will go back only to 1974–1975, which I have described as a become-aware period for most corporations. My own corporation's health care costs were 23.4 percent higher in 1975 than in 1974, the biggest escalation we had ever had. Most large companies had rates of increase in those years of over 25 percent. The health care industry came out of the freeze later than the rest of the country, and most of that increase was a result of coming out of the freeze.

The 1975–1978 period was one of lashing out, finding somebody to blame, single-minded solutions to our problems, and activities associated with simple answers—a period pretty much of going it alone. The companies solved the problems by themselves. It must be the doctors, they said, and so they talked to the doctors about their problem. They saw that 40 or 50 percent of what they paid was paid to the hospitals; the hospitals must be the culprit, then, and so they talked to the hospitals. The response from the hospitals was to listen patiently to the companies' complaints about rapidly escalating costs and then to say: "We don't understand. You are the ones who gave people first-dollar coverage, and now you come to us and ask us to control your costs." Not a bad response.

In that three-year period individual companies zeroed in on some particular aspect of the problem. Goodyear, for example, identified length of stay as the problem; if they could reduce the average hospital stay of their employees by even one day, they would save zillions of dollars. They forgot about days their people would spend in that activity. Many large companies were reacting to rapidly escalating costs by themselves, saying, "We know how to solve our problems; we have solved all the other problems this company ever had, and we can solve this one by ourselves."

The period 1979 to 1981 was a period of the formation of groups, or coalitions. A lot of data gathering went on; Penjerdel, one of the coalitions represented here today (by Roland Wetzel), has built one of the finest data bases—on health care in Philadelphia—of any coalition. A lot of self-education also went on in the coalitions and sharing of information about what their problems were. A great deal of cost shifting also occurred as companies undertook activities that did nothing about total health care costs but simply shifted costs from one company or one group of companies to another.

I would characterize the period since 1982 as a period of focus as the private sector began to look at what it had been doing, to focus on what the problems in the health care system are, and to identify as one of the problems a perverse reimbursement system.

The Washington Business Group on Health formed a task force on competition. Rather than looking at legislation, they asked, What are we trying to accomplish with competition? As Alain Enthoven's book *Health Plan* states, before we have competition, we have to have competing units. Those competing units have a different reimbursement system from fee for service in the health care system as we have known it. If we are going to do anything about the system, we have to look at ways to change the perverse way we reimburse, in which ever-increasing use is rewarded and incurs no penalties.

We have come to recognize that cost shifting is not a long-term solution; a lot of cost shifting has occurred within the private sector, in which one company has made an arrangement with a hospital to its advantage. The total costs of hospitals in the community did not decrease—their budget was unchanged, they did not lay off any people, they did not shut down any beds. Somebody else picked up the bill as a result of what one company or one coalition did.

It was in this period that the Business Roundtable entered the fray. The roundtable is the most prestigious of the business organizations, and it does not establish priorities lightly. When it does, it intends to accomplish what it sets out to do. The roundtable established health care cost escalation as one of its significant agenda items for the next two or three years.

Sean Sullivan suggested that we can classify private sector initiatives in this area as those that change the system and those that are designed to change behavior, but the private sector has come to realize that however well these individual activities are carried out, if the overall health care costs are not reduced, they are not very meaningful. We can pick any one of the activities and say that it is good and will accomplish what it set out to do—it will lower utilization, lower demand, and so on. But unless we shrink the system, lower overall expenditures, all we have done is move the cost around.

Let's take a look at what some of those activities are, because we have a group of panelists here who can expand on them. I have tried to put them in logical categories, such as short-term and long-term strategies, cost-shifting and not-cost-shifting, do-it-yourself or do-it-with-other-groups.

I start with do-it-yourself activities that really save money and do not shift costs. There are not many of those, but if your company is simply looking for ways to slow the rate of escalation of its health care costs, there is an activity the company should consider that is often overlooked. That's the wage replacement cost for personal sickness and injury. At Alcoa we spend about $10 million a year on that, about 10 percent of our total health care expenditures. When employees are off sick or injured, we pay a portion of their pay. For our salaried people we pay 100 percent of salary for a short period and then 60 percent of salary for up to two years; for hourly people we pay 50 to 60 percent of straight time. We do not give very much attention to that. An employee has a hernia operation, and in most cases we simply wait for his personal doctor to say the employee is ready to come back to work; if that is six or eight weeks later, that is when it is. There is very little challenging of whether people need to be off for that period of time. We believe that we can save at least 20 percent of wage replacement costs simply by managing, as we manage any other piece of business, by following up on those people once they are off sick or injured.

Dick Egdahl informed me of some tables that show what doctors around the country consider standard return-to-work dates after various procedures, and he described them as unconscionable. Dr. Egdahl gets his patients out of the hospital about three days after surgery, and he believes that getting them back to work early is favorable rather than unfavorable for the employee. This activity does not shift costs to anybody else or require negotiation with anybody unless a company has an agreement with a union that would prevent it from pursuing this approach, and most companies have not.

A second approach is to look at your coverage to make sure that you reimburse as well for outpatient as for inpatient services. There are still some plans under which the employee must go into the hospital to get coverage. This is another thing you probably can do by yourself, and most unions will not object because it is an alternative, not a takeaway.

You also ought to look at the way you provide coverage. If you are fully insured and are large enough to be self-funded, certainly you ought to look into self-funding. It has nothing to do with changing the health care system, and it does not shift costs; it just affects what you pay to provide coverage. Those are three rather straightforward activities that I put in the category of do-it-yourself without cost shifting.

Another category I describe as reduced-demand activities. These include such things as hospital utilization review. In Cleveland, for example, a hospital review organization was established by the business community to provide concurrent review, preferably with nonhospital employees. Another activity of the same kind is to establish the appropriate protocol for different diagnoses. It is getting at the same thing, hospital utilization review.

A second reduced-demand strategy would be to redesign first-dollar coverage plans, to introduce deductibles and copayments. If there is a trend that probably will continue, it is this activity of changing first-dollar coverage, to reduce demand by getting employees involved in the payment mechanism. First-dollar plans give the employee a free ticket to buy health care; when the doctor says he is going to put someone in the hospital, there is no consideration of cost by employees or their dependents. It's paid for; they might have to pay for long-distance phone calls—probably not even for a television, because that is generally included in the room rate. U.S. Steel, for example, found that when they introduced a hospital deductible only, similar to the Medicare deductible—it was about $200 and is now $304 with a $50 deductible for emergency room service—they experienced in the first six months a reduction of 18 percent per employee in the number of hospital admissions. The average stay went up a little bit from 6.4 to 6.7 days, but that would be expected because some short stays were eliminated. When the doctor wants to put an employee in the hospital for a couple of days for tests, the employee says, "That's going to cost me $304; can we do it some other way?" About half the companies in the Pittsburgh Business Group on Health in the last year have changed the design of their plans for either bargaining or nonbargaining people to include deductibles and copayments.

Another reduced-demand strategy is to provide for a second opinion, probably mandatory rather than voluntary; there is no evidence that a voluntary provision is used. I do not think that is a strong strategy, but some people are very enthusiastic about mandatory second opinions.

Preadmission testing and precertification constitute a lower-demand strategy. Some companies have changed their plans to require that, except in emergencies, there must be precertification for admittance to the hospital. This is simply a reduced-demand strategy. I would put education of hospital trustees in the category of reduced-utilization strategy.

Also in that category—but totally different because it is a behavior-change strategy—is the emphasis on life style or wellness. Many companies are trying to change the behavior of their employees so that they will need less health care. That is the bottom line. We can say that it is to make healthier, more productive employees, but I believe the reason my company would do it is to try to slow the escalation of health care costs. Some companies represented here can have a good bit to say about this; Kimberly-Clark was one of the early companies to take action on this issue. As we look at where our health care costs come from, we believe that $30 to $50 million of the $100 million we spend is a result of what our employees and dependents do to themselves. They were not born sick, they were not born with emphysema, obesity, stress; they were not born smoking, drinking, using drugs. Of all these things that happen to them, we think some 10 percent are due to smoking and 20 percent to drugs and alcohol. IBM, Pepsico, Kimberly-Clark, New York Bell, Xerox, Control Data, Johnson and Johnson, and R. J. Reynolds are all companies that have had significant activities within this long-term strategy.

Of all the activities I have listed, none change the system. They all operate within the existing reimbursement system. That does not mean we ought not to do them, but until we change the reimbursement system, we will not really have an impact.

I find the list of things that can be done to change the system very short. One of those is to establish alternative delivery systems, that is, systems that do have a different reimbursement scheme, such as health maintenance organizations. In the next few years there will be all kinds of variations. There are now preferred provider organizations (PPOs), and there will be other arrangements, essentially putting the providers at risk for providing health care—that will be the characteristic. The Washington Business Group on Health—about 200 of the Fortune 500 companies—decided about a year and a half ago on that as a goal. If we are ever going to get to a more competitive market, people have to have the opportunity to buy their health care from competing units.

A second way to change the reimbursement arrangement is a regulatory approach—through prospective reimbursement, through diagnostic-related groups (DRGs), through a cap on expenditures. A hospital now under Medicare, instead of being reimbursed for its costs or charges, knows in advance that it will be reimbursed $1,500 for a certain procedure, one of the 467 DRGs. Although I put those strategies in the category of moving toward a competitive marketplace, both have a strong possibility of shifting costs. You will hear more today about the private sector's concern about cost shifting if

Medicare adopts DRGs. On the one hand, we in the private sector have asked the government why it does not do something about the health care that it pays for; on the other hand, when we see what it does, it causes us concern because it may shift a lot of costs to us.

Another series of activities I call legislative activities—things that the private sector is doing, has done, or will do that relate to legislation, in the area, for example, of health planning. The private sector was concerned that the federal government would eliminate health planning before there was something to replace it; so the private sector has had some things to say about what ought to happen to health planning.

I will just list three other activities—the tax cap, unemployment insurance, and the attempt of the American Medical Association to get out from under Federal Trade Commission regulation. Those are all activities of the private sector in the last few years to do something about the nation's health care costs.

I have not talked about coalitions as an activity to do something about health care costs. The reason is that I view them as a vehicle to accomplish any of the activities I have listed, not as an activity in itself. Some coalitions are doing very good things. The Robert Wood Johnson Foundation's program on affordable health care has led a lot of communities to form broader-based coalitions than just the business coalitions. David Klein just told me that the foundation has made eleven planning grants to communities and may make as many as three or four more. I applaud the foundation for moving many communities to do something about their health care costs.

The activities I have mentioned are not mutually exclusive. You can do all of them. Although it seems a bit incompatible, you can push for prospective reimbursement in your state and at the same time pursue a competitive strategy. I don't see anything inconsistent in that. If you think that in the short term a regulatory approach is right and in the long term want a better marketplace, go for one now and work on the other later. If you have enough money and energy, I would encourage you to undertake all these activities, but I think you will find you have to decide where you can best focus your efforts. Many of those activities will be fun to do, but unless they shrink the health care system so as to reduce overall costs, they will be in vain.

MR. SULLIVAN: I would like each of our panelists to take five minutes or so either to comment on a significant aspect of what Dick Wardrop has had to say or to offer a particular perspective of their own on private sector cost containment. We will start with Dick Arnould, of the College of Commerce and Business Administration at the University of Illinois.

RICHARD ARNOULD, University of Illinois: I get paid for being an academic and economist, which makes me a little concerned about being in a format like this. But I am also a trustee of a hospital board, which has opened my eyes to another side of this issue, and do consulting with hospitals and industry, which opens still another bias.

Let me start by emphasizing two or three things that were just said. One is very pessimistic. As I talk to different groups in different places, one thing that greatly disturbs me is to blame the federal government for rising hospital costs. The blame lies just as much with private industry as with the federal government because five years ago people from private industry were not meeting in groups like this to worry about cost containment.

The whole incentive structure that government adopted for Medicare and Medicaid was part of the private industry benefits package before those federal government programs were in place. I am not saying that those programs do not need to be changed; I am saying that the private sector programs need to be changed just as much. Until we get that kind of a change in the incentive structure, we will not have much effective long-term cost containment.

Three different incentive structures are involved—the hospital, the doctor, and management and labor. I put management and labor together because this is an issue that they should not be fighting about; their incentives should be the same.

The hospital's incentive is to keep the hospital filled. The doctors' incentive is to remain under the old fee-for-service system, where they get an additional dollar for every additional unit of service they provide. At this stage of our economic development, management and labor should be worried about efficient health care plans and efficient health care. I emphasize their being together because they have one long-run goal, which is to be in business tomorrow, next year, and ten years from now. The Rolls Royce health care plan does not help the guy who is not employed at all. We are hearing now in Washington about legislation to provide some kind of health insurance for the long-term unemployed.

We had an interesting situation in our own hospital, where we have an affiliated clinic, with about 150 tertiary and primary care doctors. We are located about fifty miles from Danville, Illinois, which is very different from Champaign-Urbana. Champaign-Urbana is a university town; Danville is a smokestack town, almost totally heavy industry, with widespread unemployment. When a corporation that employed approximately 1,200 people there considered moving the plant somewhere in the South, the union asked to become a part of the HMO in our clinic. Why did they do that? Did that reduce the cost of the health care? It didn't reduce it very much if at all, but it provided a guaranteed price for the health care benefits package, and it gave that company a change in the reimbursement structure that provided incentives for efficient delivery of health care. We moved into that community with a satellite, starting with three physicians three days a week; the schedules were filled by the end of the first week. We are now increasing the staff to about five physicians and building a full clinical outpatient facility in that hospital.

Will change come about? It will come about, I think, for a number of reasons. One is simply the kind of thing that happened to us. Why did they come to a clinic forty or fifty miles away rather than stay in town? The doctors in Danville had an organization that, as we saw it, had one thing in mind—to remain unorganized. There was no organized package that group could or would put together or was willing to consider until we moved into town. They are now meeting frequently to figure out how to set up their own individual practice association (IPA), how to get an organization that will keep more of the industry from going away from the local physician.

The incentive for change is there, and it is coming about because of a number of things. One is private sector pressures. Within the last two or three years, private industries have become aware of how much they are paying for health care for employees. Why this just happened two or three years ago I don't really know because they have been paying a lot of money for a lot of years. Because you in private industry are large-scale buyers, you have many ways to exert pressure, and you should use them.

On the supply side, things are changing rapidly. Doctors are now going through what lawyers went through ten or fifteen years ago—excess supply. An editorialist in the *New York Times* came up with the solution to two problems—the surplus lawyer problem and the balance-of-payments problem—that before another Japanese automobile could be brought into the United States, Japan had to agree to accept a lawyer. We are getting there with doctors; whether or not doctors want to organize, whether or not they want to realize what is happening in the market, they will do so because of the supply. We now comment monthly at board meetings about specialists that have moved into the little town down the road. That little town at best had a G.P., and all the referrals from that G.P. automatically came to us. Now there may be a cardiologist, there may be a urologist, there may be all kinds of specialists in that small community. The cities have for quite a while had an excess supply of doctors and unfilled schedules, but they are coming all over the country now.

Another factor is the oversupply of hospital beds. Hospitals are going to have to figure out what to do with those empty floors in many cities around the country. I cannot speak for the cities here, but I know Chicago is highly overbuilt and our local community is heavily overbuilt. Certificate-of-need controls have been extremely ineffective in controlling capital expenditures efficiently. The change must come about through changing the incentives, which will come about through changing the reimbursement system, which will come about because another group of providers in town sets up a mechanism that is more appealing to the buyer or the buyer forces that change on them.

Another thing that Mr. Wardrop mentioned was the education of hospital trustees. That is an excellent suggestion, and doctors ought to be included. It is amazing how many hospitals operate on the grounds that when they need something they will have a fund drive and that will build the new hospital. Fortunately, our hospital has an excellent administrator who believes that, with the amount of capital invested in our facility, it should be run as much as possible like a for-profit institution. That means being concerned not only with revenues but with costs, with what rate of return is needed on that investment to keep it up and to keep up with technology. That kind of education, particularly for the hospital trustees and administrators and doctors, is very effective.

I think the change is going to come, but it has not come yet. The competition we see is minimal. We typically hear from the health care community that incentives raise the issue of quality versus cost containment. You people in industry who have had to compete since the beginning know that quality and cost containment go hand in hand. You establish a level of quality and produce that level of quality that the market demands most efficiently. That does not mean that there will be one quality sold in the market. You find different qualities, the different niches that the market warrants.

The health industry has a very severe malpractice problem, a problem that I do not know how to solve. Before I was a hospital trustee, I thought it was a highly exaggerated problem, but now I do not see it as much exaggerated—it is highly significant. When you get into cost containment, you have to worry about that. But the incentive structure and the pressures have to come from the buyer and from the natural market pressures through increased supply on the seller side.

MR. SULLIVAN: I will now ask Bob Dedmon, one of three M.D.s at the table today, who comes to us as a representative of the health services center at the Kimberly-Clark Corporation, to present his perspective on our subject.

ROBERT E. DEDMON, Kimberly-Clark Corporation: I should tell you that I work both sides of the street. I come from a background of private practice in internal medicine and for the last six years have been corporate medical director of Kimberly-Clark. It has been said that all of us want to go to heaven but none of us want to die, and that is the situation in the containment of health care costs—there are many constituencies or groups, none of which really want to give up anything.

One of the approaches mentioned by Dick Wardrop is that of prevention—the wellness or life-style change approach—and that is what Kimberly-Clark has been involved in for approximately six years. Kimberly-Clark has a health management program, which has four components. The first is medical screening and health risk assessment with counseling for life-style change. The second is physical fitness, with an in-house exercise facility and one of the few in-house cardiac rehabilitation programs in the United States. The third is a variety of health education classes, and the fourth is an employee assistance program for alcohol, drug abuse, and other special personal health problems. We are attempting to change the behavior and the culture of our work force and their dependents. We also hope to have some effect on the behavior of physicians, but our primary targets are our employees, their dependents, and our retired employees.

The screening is free to all participants, but the participants pay for health education classes, and their spouses pay $100 a year to participate in the program. The program is available to employees, retirees, and their spouses in the Fox Valley area of Wisconsin, which is our headquarters area; we also have a smaller program in our group headquarters in Roswell, Georgia; and we are starting in a small way to introduce modified versions of our fitness programs in some of our new mills being constructed in Paris, Texas, and La Grange, Georgia. Our employee assistance program is being implemented in all our mill locations throughout the United States and Canada, and the National High Blood Pressure Month promotion program is in place in all our units in the United States and Canada.

In 1977 the program was made available to salaried employees only in the Fox Valley area. In 1979 it was made available to hourly employees—incidentally, this was not a negotiated item—and in January 1982 it was opened to spouses and retirees. We grew from forty visits a year to our exercise facility in 1978 to over 80,000 visits in 1982, but we still have only about a 20 to 25 percent participation rate in our

32,000-square-foot exercise facility, which comprises a twenty-five-meter, five-lane pool, a suspended indoor running track, saunas, a whirlpool, a locker room, showers, and an exercise equipment room with bicycles, weights, treadmill, universal weight machine, and so forth; we also have an outdoor track. I have a staff of twenty-three full- and part-time employees, which includes one other full-time physician besides myself, nurses, technicians, a health educator, and other staff.

We also have an in-house training program for undergraduate and graduate students in adult health and fitness, recreation management, and so on, so that they can complete three months' practical experience. We have had students from a number of universities in that program for periods of one to three months. They participate without pay, and the demand for that program is growing all the time.

I have not shown any change yet in health care costs or absenteeism. When we took a sample of people a year before they went into treatment for alcoholism and a year after, however, we found a 43 percent reduction in absenteeism and a 70 percent reduction in accidents. We have had projections that we would get a payback on our employee assistance program in three years and on our health and fitness program in seven years; I have not been able to show that, and I believe it will take at least ten years to show results. We have conducted over 1,500 tours since we opened, and consultants are constantly after me to give them results. When I told one of them that it would take us at least ten years to get a payback on this program, he said, "That's unacceptable. I have to tell the management of this company they're going to get a payback in two years." And I replied, "If you tell them that and convince them of that, they're going to be sorely disappointed."

This is a long-term investment. It has been very good for employee relations, it certainly has helped corporate recruiting, and it has had spinoff in the community. One family practitioner left his private practice, opened a private version of what we are trying to do in the community, and is being moderately successful.

There are some problems. The biggest problem is how to get people motivated and keep them motivated to persist in the program, and we are constantly looking at ways to do that. There are no direct financial incentives in the program.

The second problem is what I call the problem of the myth. There are two principal myths—the white-collar myth and the blue-collar myth. The blue-collar myth is that because I wear overalls and do not wear a necktie to work, I am doing heavy physical labor. I know of no heavy physical labor job at Kimberly-Clark except for our lumberjacks in Canada and Alabama. Most of the work in the mills is automated; occasionally people have to do some lifting. But that is an American cultural myth—blue collar equals hard physical work—that is no longer true. Another problem with blue-collar workers is that their life style is largely sedentary. The Minnesota Heart Program has addressed this problem with an objective to get blue-collar workers into some kind of exercise program as an alternative to television. The white-collar myth goes something like this: it will never happen to us. Professional people, physicians, scientists, managers, and so on who have certain ego structures think they can do whatever they like and not get a heart attack or cancer. It is particularly true in the area of alcohol and drug abuse, although legions of people can testify otherwise who have gone through bad experiences one way or another.

Another problem is how to get along with the medical community and keep the doctors from getting mad at us for taking business away from them. I came from the medical community and joined Kimberly-Clark full time. It helped that I was in private practice in internal medicine, and we have had very few problems with the physicians. In fact, our screening program has increased their business, at least the cardiologist business and the oncologist business. We have a very good working relationship with the medical community.

Our chief executive officer believes the program has paid for itself already. The people he knows in the program stand the stress of their work better, they look better, he thinks they feel better, and they are more productive. When I talk at medical meetings about this, physicians always ask how I persuaded management to do it and always have trouble believing that I didn't: the senior management decided to do it and persuaded me to join the program. At fifty pounds lighter, I'm very happy that I did.

MR. SULLIVAN: The president of one corporation instituted an incentive program for participation in the kind of fitness activities you describe, with bonus points for miles swum, miles run, and miles cycled. In the first year of the program, the president himself earned 25 percent of the total bonus paid; so a dedicated CEO had a lot to do with getting these programs going. Our next speaker is Bill Goldbeck, who runs the Washington Business Group on Health.

WILLIS B. GOLDBECK, Washington Business Group on Health: I have three points, which perhaps can be expanded upon later in the discussion.

The first is to emphasize the severity of the problem. This issue is not going to go away, it is not going to be wished away. That we have been lying about the problems of Medicare, pretending about them, for the past ten years is symptomatic of another set of national problems, which are not going to be addressed in the health care sector; we should no longer ignore that we have an uncovered population nearly equal to the number of uncovered persons that drove this nation within one vote of national health insurance in 1975 with the Kennedy-Mills bill. We have an access problem as well as a cost problem once again.

Second, the severity of the change should be noted. We are virtually eliminating traditional health insurance in the United States. The concept of a national approach through a variety of private sector and some public sector sources that set a norm and spread the risk of that norm over very large groups is to a large degree defunct today, and all the attempts to trim costs are making it more so. The more we negotiate, the more we segment; the more we get people into alternative mechanisms "appropriate" for their immediate health care needs, the more those who have the paramount needs are left picking up what used to be the high-option or normal plan, and everybody else selects himself or herself into interesting and appropriate and perhaps less expensive buckets. The traditional methodology is virtually gone, and we should recognize that, because much of the dialogue about how to fix the system is predicated on fixing a system that virtually no longer exists.

Third is the change in the doctor-hospital relationship—whether it is through diagnostic-related groups (DRGs) or any other method—the day of the medical staff's dictating to the hospital is fast approaching its end. Hospitals will be dictating practice patterns, will be hiring and controlling entry, in ways that had not even been conceived of as recently as two or three years ago. General societal recognition that the doctor is increasingly not the omnipotent force is certainly significant, as is the growing recognition that hospitals themselves are not inherently good. Granted some communities have not come to that point yet, but more and more have. As various programs prove effective in lessening occupancy rates, the lack of validity of individual institutions will become increasingly apparent. It is relatively easy to argue that our hospital or our eighth hospital in town is essential when it has an 85 percent occupancy rate. After the appropriate programs are put in place through competition, regulation, or both and we find that the legitimate rate is 45 percent, the initial argument is undermined. It takes a while for the action to catch up to deal with the capacity, but unless we build in the activities that produce the evidence of the necessity for change, the change will never come about.

We must also come to grips with the fact that the severity of this problem combined with the pressure from technology will result in increasingly explicit rationing of technology over the next decade in the United States. I don't think there is any way to avoid it, and it will probably be the greatest ethical dilemma that this country has ever publicly confronted.

All of this seems to me to be connected to a set of changing values. One is that the decision-making process, whether for individuals or for management, labor, or governmental units, is changing from an acquiescence mode to an information or selection mode, in which people are gaining increased access to comparative facts. We are beginning to replace the legal construct of freedom of choice with the practical construct of meaningful choice, of people being able to select among providers about whom they know something rather than about whom only myths and rumors exist. Second, it is now deemed appropriate that management, labor, and the user ought to manage jointly something that is in fact a part of compensation. This was not true a few years ago: "You don't manage the rest of the dollars in the pay envelope together; why should you manage this?" was the attitude. It is becoming increasingly evident why you had better manage it, and not only for cost reasons; if it is not a managed asset, people are left to thrash about in a system that is not really designed for their benefit. Third is the changing value that government, labor, and business are natural allies on this issue. Fourth, quality enhancement need not be contrary to cost control. If we look at any of the statistics on the appropriateness of care setting, we see that we can cut out a significant portion of today's hospital system and only improve the quality of care for people who get care in other settings. That is equally true if we improve the quality of corporate programs, although that is not an essential result.

Related to that is the point I mentioned earlier on adverse selection. We must not lose sight of the fact that almost every one of the positive things that we are talking about will produce an increasingly explicitly defined population for whom the system will no longer be designed. We don't know what to do about that; we really don't even want to talk about it.

Another element or indication of changing values is the way we are inextricably marching toward national standards, which are probably long overdue and not nearly as prescriptive as they might sound. National standards in medical practice need not mean that any surgeon has to cut like any other surgeon. It does mean that there are certain ranges and norms that are perfectly comprehensible, both by laymen and by professionals, that these standards can be measured, and that there is no inherent reason why the practice of medicine should be practiced 180 degrees differently, with no difference in outcome, in one town from another. The variations that exist today are not justifiable by medicine, by quality of care, and certainly not by cost management.

In the next ten years we will see a tremendous shift in orientation toward the appropriateness of self-care and an emphasis on emotional and mental health. If we do not come to grips with that, we will have missed the prime technological instrument for affecting the body system, and it is not one you can buy in a store.

My final point is to note that much of what has been and will be discussed today is evidence of a growing sophistication of the leaders in the buyer community—not the norm; in the business community followers are the norm just as they are in the health, medicine, public policy, or any other community. The leaders are recognizing the appropriateness and indeed the necessity of a strategy of integrating wellness with the rest of benefits rather than looking at them as separate and are recognizing that employees are really not the statistical issue, that dependents and retirees are by far the larger consumers of benefits. All the efforts of the past five or ten years that have addressed employees almost exclusively are merely the harbinger of a transfer of that effort to the larger-scale users, the dependents and retirees. Bethlehem Steel now has more than one covered retiree for every active worker. That is the trend. We cannot ignore involving retirees in the active participation of cost management programs.

On the comments that have been made about teaching employees to manage their stress, their stress is our stress because we the company in many respects gave it to them and are continuing to do so. We will deal only with work-site stress when we deal with the stressees and the stressers in tandem.

The emphasis on negotiated agreements will fail in the absence of a greatly increased sophistication on the part of the corporate negotiator. Discounts are not the answer except to fatten the possible profits of the providers. Competition and regulation must be viewed as a joint effort rather than as competing efforts.

We must understand that a delayed payoff is appropriate. Dick Wardrop mentioned that Deere has reduced its utilization in Illinois and Iowa by an average of about 33 percent and has seen virtually no change in the cost per capita of the hospitalized patient. That is appropriate, it is not a failure; it is the beginning of a success, because the change of the capacity of the system has to follow, not lead, the change in the use of the system where there is a system already in place. We must understand the importance of changing the system and recognize that cost shifting has various components and is not a single item. Finally, a great many employers now understand that they will not succeed in cost management unless they make the individual employee, dependent, and retiree a partner in that effort. Employers cannot succeed alone in this venture any more than government could.

MR. SULLIVAN: Our next speaker is the second M.D. on our panel, Ron Henderson, of the Council on Medical Service of the American Medical Association.

RONALD E. HENDERSON, American Medical Association: I come to you as a member of the Council on Medical Service of the American Medical Association, which deals with socioeconomic issues. The AMA has had an interest in the cost of medical care since 1966 because we saw then the major threat to the health of this nation as being not the accessibility of care or the quality of care but the cost. Coming out of that interest was a corporate visitation program by the AMA, and from that came a national planning committee in which the AMA joined with five or six national companies, such as Ford, Exxon, Citibank, Aetna, and U.S. Steel, to address the problem of escalating costs. The initial plan of the national planning committee was to have five pilot projects, one of which was the Birmingham, Alabama, steering committee, of which I am a founding member.

Birmingham was targeted because of the high utilization rates of the U.S. Steel employees in Birmingham as contrasted to the rest of the plants across the country. We started meeting in 1979, and we have a success story to tell. The coalitions are vehicles for other activities, and that is exactly the way we view our efforts in Birmingham. We have approached the issue from several aspects. We have had data collection; we have had efforts to change the way physicians practice and the way they use health care institutions; we have tried to design a prototype plan with built-in disincentives to utilization and to change the system so that there is more reimbursement for outpatient facilities—preadmission testing for inpatients and a thrust toward outpatient ambulatory surgery. We have also had a focus on wellness programs.

On the basis of the number of patient-days per thousand insured in the Birmingham Blue Cross–Blue Shield program, we are among the top users in the nation. The first impact that we hoped to make was on the 1982 data. In recent data for the first six months of 1982, we see several encouraging signs. In the companies that did not have major layoffs during the recession, utilization seems to have decreased. In the companies that did terminate major groups of employees, use of continued health insurance coverage increased. We think this result is a fluke brought on by the system. We have seen decreased Friday and Saturday admissions; therefore, we think that the medical society, working with the business groups, has been instrumental in changing physicians' patterns. We are very encouraged about what future data will show. I would encourage you, if you are involved in a coalition, not to point fingers or fix blame. It is important to look at the whole system and not focus exclusively on any one aspect.

We now have nationally some 147 coalitions with various makeups. About 21 percent of them are business owned, but we do not feel that they are really coalitions; a broader base is needed to be effective. About 113 of the 147 have medical society participation, which we feel is a proper way to go.

MR. SULLIVAN: Our next speaker will be David Klein of Blue Cross–Blue Shield, which is involved in a wide range of activities.

DAVID KLEIN, Blue Cross and Blue Shield: The issues before this group are certainly deserving of attention. They take on increasing significance as you look at the profile of expenses in your companies and typically see that the highest variance from year to year is in health benefits.

We have heard repeatedly that the incentives in the existing system were effective in promoting high-quality medical care and in promoting access. The time has now come to moderate some of those incentives to orient them to cost containment. We are looking for an integration of financing and delivery. The changes will be pluralistic, will be incremental. They will be locally developed to recognize the varied health care delivery system that exists, one that integrates high-capacity areas with low-capacity areas, areas that have multiple hospitals with areas that have single hospitals, areas that have many specialists with areas that do not.

Changes must recognize a segmentation in the market. This is a very important variable. Just as the automobile manufacturers give us both Cadillacs and Chevettes, a spectrum of health care products must be available for employers to purchase from time to time. We must allow for differences in employers' capacities. We have heard that the changes will have both short-term and long-term orientations. The imperative for individual employers is to invest in the long rather than in the short term. Both kinds of changes must be contemplated. We have heard that both regulatory and market-oriented approaches will be undertaken, probably both effectively, probably decided on locally. We have heard that some of the solutions may shift the contribution made by the various purchasers of care. We are talking about different contributions to the operating margins of suppliers, no different from what we see in many industries: consider a convention in a hotel and whether the convention program directors are paying the same rate for a room as the man on the street, or a steel company buying steel versus a small supplier buying steel. There are deserved differentials. There is no panacea, no simple solution; each solution has to be custom designed to the problems in each local environment for each employer.

Blue Cross–Blue Shield plans are a pervasive force in this industry. There are ninety-eight plans, locally owned and operated, with 80 million members. We integrate ourselves into the design and execution of these solutions and are typically considered allies by our communities and our accounts. There is hardly an activity described here today that we are not involved with—changes in the design of benefit plans; cost sharing; cost containment; plan administration; coordination of benefit programs; bill audit programs; medical necessity programs (we have done some pioneering work there, working with medical specialty societies on medical procedures that are obsolete or should be brought into question from time to time); fraud and abuse control programs; utilization review programs involving preadmission certification; concurrent review; working with the professional standards review organizations (PSROs) and without them; working with foundations for medical care and working without them; life-style programs, wellness programs, and substance abuse programs; contractual arrangements with hospitals and doctors to give them incentives to behave as they should, though maybe not always as effectively as we would like; health planning support; reports to accounts regarding the cost utilization patterns of their employees; support of health maintenance organizations; and alternative delivery systems. We own fifty-seven HMOs across the country with 1 million members. As I list those activities, I am not impressed by their innovativeness. In many ways, they are the conventional system.

In many places across the country we are working toward channeling employees to use more cost-effective providers, providers we would prefer to give business to. This movement is being called a preferred provider system. It fits into the two specific areas I have mentioned: the notion of market segmentation and the notion of alternative delivery systems. The research that we have done suggests that employees are willing to sacrifice access for price reduction, to be channeled to particular hospitals and particular doctors provided that they are not foreclosed from other hospitals or other doctors if they need care from somebody who is not on a preferred panel.

In a survey done a few weeks ago, we found that seventeen Blue Cross and Blue Shield plans are developing preferred provider products, products that would channel patients to particular hospitals or doctors that we believe will engender more effective price and use patterns. Another forty report that they are facing decisions on whether such a product should be developed. Three plans are selling such products. Minnesota has a program called Aware (from cost awareness); Blue Cross of California has a prudent buyer program; and the Richmond, Virginia, plan has a program called Key Care. These programs are different from one another except that a selection has been made of less than the full universe of providers and some sort of incentive has been provided: reduced coverage if the patient goes to a nonpreferred provider, so as to channel more patients to preferred providers.

The Minnesota program uses a fairly simple cost reduction technique. An offer was made to the twenty-seven hospitals in the greater Minneapolis–St. Paul area, to which twenty responded positively, for a per diem payment set at the fifty-fifth percentile. That panel of hospitals includes a number of the tertiary care centers. There has been no sacrifice in quality of service. We have added a length-of-stay incentive; if length of stay drops, a bonus will be paid to the hospitals, and if length of stay increases, a penalty will be paid by the hospital.

In Richmond, Virginia, a similar approach was used, although there was not a single price posted for all institutions. There was some customization, to recognize that in certain cases, especially among tertiary care hospitals or in certain parts of that metropolitan area where there was a lower-cost provider, an arrangement would have to be made for an incremental payment. Ten of the fourteen providers in the greater Richmond area have signed contracts to be Key Care providers.

In California the work began as a response to Medi-Cal (the California Medicaid program) legislation that was passed last summer, which named a Medi-Cal czar to negotiate and contract for the care of Medi-Cal patients. Predicated on that experience, the plan recently asked for bids from 159 hospitals for care to be rendered, received bids from 144, and selected 42 of them. There is not a standard price for all the institutions, but the price is based on the bid made by the individual institution. Those 42 hospitals are located in about half a dozen counties, and the intention is to make the program statewide. Again they include tertiary care institutions.

The price differential on all three of these products has been about 7 to 10 percent at the outset, and we think we have been conservative in our rating. Whether you want to call this a short-term or a medium-term intervention, it is clearly an alternative delivery system, which recognizes the market segment that is willing to sacrifice timely access.

MR. SULLIVAN: Our next speaker is Lindy Saline, who, though on the program as from the General Electric Company, is here perhaps more as the roving ambassador and spokesman for the Business Roundtable's Health Care Cost Committee.

LINDON SALINE, General Electric Company: I would like to describe very briefly the Business Roundtable health initiatives, which have been joined by 160 of the 200 roundtable member companies. With that kind of involvement, we potentially affect 13 million employees, 5 million retirees, and over 30 million dependents, all together more than 20 percent of the U.S. population.

The goals for the health initiatives are straightforward—to provide high-quality, accessible, and affordable health care. We operate on the premise that, contrary to the no-fault mentality that pervades our society, everybody is guilty of contributing to the health care cost increase, not the least business, which has tolerated, contributed to, and encouraged the development of the health care system.

Our approach to doing something about that health care system has three main thrusts. The first is to eliminate waste in the management of the system; the second is to focus on individual responsibility; and the third is to do something directly and indirectly about the structure of the system. By that I mean any of a range of diverse factors, such as third-party reimbursement, alternative delivery systems, cost shifting and hospital management, planning and capital budgeting, and the cost and financing of medical education.

To implement those three thrusts, we have developed a seven-element model that we are working to implement within the roundtable companies. I will describe them now essentially by title only and can elaborate later in any degree you would like.

The first element is to help managers become aware of the health care system, both within the country and within their specific company, and also to help them understand that health care is manageable. The second is to encourage companies to establish a high-quality claims data base. The third is to use that data base and claims data analysis in utilization review. The fourth is to give attention to health promotion and safety on and away from the job. The fifth is to make a thorough review of the health plan itself. The sixth is to stress communication and education to help employees understand their personal responsibility for—and the influence of their life-style decisions on—their health and to help them become better health care consumers and buyers. Another thrust of the education program is directed to business managers, who should focus more effectively on workers' compensation management and on control of absenteeism. The seventh element has to do with community activities, and these have four aspects: first, to encourage business executives to be effective trustees of institutions in the health care system; second, to help businesses understand the dangers of counterproductive health care philanthropy; third, to get involved in legislative and regulative issues at the local, state, and federal levels; and fourth, to participate actively in local health coalitions.

How are we doing in all of this? We learned a long time ago that to eat an elephant, you do it one bite at a time. So we are not trying to do all things immediately; rather we are chipping away in a systematic way that will be sustained. In the fifteen months that I have been involved in this activity, I have noticed quite a difference in the interest and effectiveness of large companies, at least in taking health care management more seriously and more effectively. I notice that carriers and providers are becoming more responsive to the needs of businesses for claims data and are responding to the utilization reviews that are being conducted. Companies are becoming much more serious about helping employees lead better lives and get all the benefits thereof.

MR. SULLIVAN: We will now go to a different perspective, which will be given us by Cathy Schoen, who is here representing the Service Employees International Union (SEIU) and also representing Karen Ignagni of the AFL-CIO.

CATHY SCHOEN, SEIU: Karen Ignagni apologizes for not being here and has asked me to use some non-SEIU examples. I want to start a bit more broadly than the topic for today, which was new models for cost containment, and to point out that there is still an access problem in the United States. One of the things we tend to forget when we talk about public and private initiatives for cost shifting is that we are going to pay, one way or another, for the population that is currently unemployed or retired. We will pay through taxes or through cost shifting in our hospital bills or through something very few commentators on the cost shift have noticed. Medicaid programs around the country are cutting back on all the preventive care and primary care services. We find increasing instances of premature babies with low birth weights, which could have been prevented with adequate prenatal care and nutrition; one of our health plans spent $60,000, $80,000, and $100,000 for three very sick infants of employees. After their hospitalization the babies became wards of the state as well and were placed in institutions for the retarded.

This is a trend around the country that is going to come back to us as taxpayers because we instituted no cost-effective budget restraints in the public sector, looking at the tax dollars rather than at the system as a health care system and what kinds of services should be covered. The current statistics are a little hazy on how many are uninsured, but in 1978 a survey by the National Center for Health Services Research found that during a given year 35 million people were uninsured at some point, and this was before the recent unemployment rates. We now have another 10 million unemployed people without health insurance, and we currently employed people are paying for those people in our health care bills. That is part of this thing called cost shift. It is trying to continue providing health care for people who may not have private health insurance.

The second point I want to talk about is something we are increasingly facing, and that is an adversarial relationship on the part of management toward unions about cost containment that need not be there at all. The attitude seems to be that the first thing one does about controlling health care costs and premiums is to shift costs to the employees. This clearly will lower premium costs but may or may not do anything about total costs of care. This attitude is serving to block some very innovative programs to lower overall costs because the union has never been brought in, nor employees generally.

The kinds of blockages we are running across are straight information—what is the cost of our plan? It will be very hard to argue with any employee group that the costs of health care are too high when you refuse to tell them how much you are paying. When we ask why the premium goes up or how much of our insurance carriers' overhead we pay and get "We have no idea" as an answer, our response is, "Why is the first thing you want to do to put in a high deductible and high copayments if you have no idea?" There ought to be some analyses of what the cost problems are in a plan and joint efforts to bring those costs under control.

SEIU and several other labor unions have long had jointly managed labor-management trust funds in the private sector, and one of the advantages is that we had a vehicle in which to work jointly with our employers on cost problems. One of our locals in New York got hit in 1975 with a 50 percent increase in premiums that they could not afford; the workers represented by that plan are low-wage workers, and they could not absorb that kind of premium increase. We worked jointly to put in a set of cost containment efforts that were billed as improved benefits. They were not billed as a deduction in benefits, takebacks, or concessions, but as an expansion of benefits that was going to be cost effective overall. The plan for which we were quoted a 50 percent increase in 1975 has not yet reached that 50 percent increase in 1983 but is just approaching it. So there has been a dramatic turnaround in costs, and it has not been seen as a benefit cut.

Similarly, in Oregon, the public employees, also an SEIU local, bargained about three or four years ago for joint control over their health plan. Last year they were faced with a 54 percent increase in premiums from August 1982 through August of 1983. They put in a range of cost containment programs, only one of which was a slight cutback in benefits—a two-doctor-visits deductible. The rest were changes in the package of benefits to encourage ambulatory care and closer scrutiny of claims. The plan is going to come in at a 27 percent increase for the year instead of 54 percent, and next year's increase is going to be 6 to 7 percent—again, a dramatic turnaround through a cooperative effort.

A specific example of how a program can be communicated as working together and improving benefits or as "this is a penalty and we're going to take it out of your hide" is the mandatory second opinion for surgery. When we put this program into our plan, we billed it as a protection for employees against unnecessary surgery. Especially where we have large female bargaining units, it goes over very well to talk about the rate of unnecessary surgery, how surgery rates are increasing. Women, who undergo two-thirds of the surgery, have a lot of fear of unnecessary surgery. That program communicated in that way gets a fair amount of participation as a new benefit in the program rather than a cost containment program. In another plan the employer brought in a second opinion surgery program without much consultation, without much effort to communicate or explain. If the second doctor does not confirm the first doctor, that plan pays only 50 percent of the cost of care. Our program does not work that way. When the second opinion does not confirm, the employee can make a choice, and the effect has been dramatic in lowering surgery rates just by requiring a second opinion. The penalty situation has the employee bargaining unit up in arms. Is the plan going to be liable when an employee has needed surgery and the insurance carrier says it is not liable? That employer's approach turned an effective program into a program that everyone is fighting to resist.

Another kind of program that particularly requires cooperation is on-site workplace delivery of health care programs, which has proved especially effective in preventive care. We are running workplace hypertension clinics that both diagnose whether a person has high blood pressure and give treatment at the worksite or in clinics located at an easy access point. The first statistics on the long-term effects of this are just coming out of the store workers' union in New York, where they have had workplace clinics for about ten years. They have reduced death and hospital rates by almost half over a control group that was referred to community physicians, partly because people stay in the program—the easy access keeps them going in for blood pressure checks. The first look at the cost side shows a clear saving on the amount of money paid for hypertension care. The clinics are run by nurses with backup from physicians, and we are paying less overall than we would for hypertension care. The store workers are doing a study to see how the fewer hospital days and greater longevity translate on the cost side; these groups were carefully controlled, and there are no differences in any health statistics other than the cardiovascular. The program works because the employees are involved. They perceived it as an additional benefit. They were told not that they were responsible for their own high blood pressure and it was up to them to do something about it but that high blood pressure is an undetected problem, an asymptomatic problem that people may not be aware they have. It has been very successful in bringing people in.

In wellness programs it is important not to tell people that they are destroying their bodies in a willful way. Studies have found that occupational stress and environmental hazards and workplace hazards are far more telling in actual health statistics than individual behavior. Initially black lung was attributed to workers' behavior, until it was found that maybe it was not just that all mine workers smoke more than the rest of the population. It had something to do with the workplace. Studies have shown that clerical work, low-skilled work in dead-end jobs, is far more likely to lead to heart attacks than some of the higher-skilled, high-level executive jobs. So the structure of the workplace itself has something to do with health care as well as how often we jog or how often we swim.

We tend to look at our own small plans and try to figure out what to do in that environment, and there is certainly a lot we can do there; but we immediately come up against a system of care in the community, the state, or the nation. It is important not to fragment our horizons so that we worry about our employees, but not when they retire or go on unemployment, and do not worry about anyone else's. Some communities are now working in coalitions to find community-wide solutions. Others are trying to shift costs to one another and doing the kinds of things that a health planner would say do not constitute a rational hospital system. A rational system is not every hospital vying for patients but hospitals starting to share services. We need to put pressure as purchasers, as business and labor, and as retired and unemployed workers on the system to rationalize itself. We don't need to make it worse by fragmenting it.

MR. SULLIVAN: Our next speaker is Peter Singer, head of the Utah Health Cost Management Foundation, which I classify as a coalition, but it is a different kind of group from most of the business coalitions I have encountered.

PETER F. SINGER, Utah Health Cost Management Foundation: The Utah foundation is an all-party coalition; the board is dominated by business people, but there are also representatives from unions, physicians, hospitals, and two branches of state government. The foundation has adopted a competitive strategy from the outset. It does not necessarily believe that we do not need some regulation, at least until market forces are present, but it has focused on competition as its only strategy, primarily because no one else is focusing on it, at least at the state level. Its first priority has been to promote high-quality alternative delivery systems in Utah. We believe that these offer the greatest promise because they change the incentives of providers as well as consumers, and they seem to be the best way to wake up the fee-for-service sector, which in most states is asleep.

We have engaged in several activities, the first of which is education of providers. We have tried to demonstrate to them that it is in their best financial interests to develop and participate in alternative delivery systems. We have also given technical assistance to provider groups that have started to develop such systems. In technical assistance I include marketing and financial feasibility surveys, patient origin studies, and so on. We have also done some brokering between provider groups and national HMO firms. The critical ingredient in most alternative delivery systems is quality management, which the national HMO firms can provide.

We have also attempted to eliminate some legal obstacles to preferred provider plans in Utah. An antidiscrimination section in the Utah code effectively prevents an insurer from offering a preferred provider organization (PPO). Self-insurers are not subject to that law and can offer PPOs. We have tried in two sessions of the Utah legislature to get this law changed and will continue to do so, but it is fairly discouraging. The power of the local medical community is incredible, and we still have been unable to get the support necessary to defeat that lobby.

The other side of the alternative delivery system coin is to encourage employers to offer these systems and to evaluate them and improve their quality, and we have spent a fair amount of time trying to educate employers about the concept and their role. Over the last three years we have seen significant development of alternative delivery systems in Utah; Blue Cross–Blue Shield of Utah and Deseret Mutual Benefit Association have developed HMOs that now enroll 45,000 patients, and two national HMO firms are negotiating with provider groups in Salt Lake to develop an HMO. Perhaps most significant is the imminent development of a preferred provider plan by a large hospital chain in Utah; it expects to come on line in January 1984. That PPO will be offered only to the self-insurance community in Utah because of the antidiscrimination law.

The second area we have tried to focus on is more of a short-term strategy in that it does not affect the economic incentives of providers or consumers. It includes two benefit administration strategies, the first of which is prior authorization or precertification of elective hospital admissions and the second is mandatory second opinions. The literature is quite clear that both these programs can be effective. Our role has been twofold. We have first tried to encourage the offering of these services to private payers by local groups in Salt Lake. Recently the Utah professional standards review organizations (PSRO) decided to offer both a mandatory second opinion program and a prior authorization program to private payers. Another private entity has entered the market, which we hope will give the PSROs some decent competition. To promote the development of high-quality benefit administration programs, we have specified the requirements for effective programs. There are good second opinion programs and there are bad second opinion programs, and it is important that purchasers know what constitutes a good program.

A third area we have worked in is plan design. We provide technical assistance and consultation to employers and insurers on how to improve the design of their benefit packages. We have encouraged cost sharing and other consumer incentives and bonuses in the design of insurance plans.

The fourth area is consumer education. It is critically important to educate consumers on how to become more informed purchasers. It is not enough to give them an incentive to shop; we must give them some information to shop with. We have published ten consumer information pamphlets on health and life styles, how to choose a doctor, how to choose a hospital, surgical care, and so on. Another pamphlet gives comparative prices by hospital for the twenty-five most common surgical procedures.

A last area we have worked on, not as successfully as other areas, is the analysis of data for insurers and employers. We have two purposes. One is to identify the low-cost and high-cost providers so that insurers and employers can steer patients to low-cost providers, and the other is to identify specific problem areas within insurance plans. The major problem has been the lack of a uniform, consistent data base. We hope that with the implementation of the uniform bill in January 1984 many of our data problems will be resolved.

In conclusion, there are some very positive developments in Utah. There is a lot of opposition, however, to the concept of competition. Very few health care providers want anything to do with competition over price. That is not really unexpected: not very many people really like to compete on price. The insurance community and the business community have been going through a process of education, first realizing that they have a problem, second realizing that they have a role to play in it, and third—and perhaps most difficult—figuring out exactly what to do. Playing the role of the prudent purchaser in health care is difficult for private as well as public purchasers, and it will be a very slow process if it succeeds at all.

MR. SULLIVAN: I am going to say just a word on behalf of Dick Van Bell, of Deere and Company, because he cannot be with us. Deere is a leader in containment of health care costs in the private sector. Dick Van Bell was the manager of health care for Deere, and he is now the director of health care with a much larger span of authority—reporting to him will be medical directors and the entire part of the corporation that is concerned with health care. That is an example of the kind of internal organizational commitment that Deere and other companies are making to manage health care costs. A lot can be done by individual companies or through coalitions such as Deere is involved in, working at the local level.

Deere's utilization review has had a great deal of success in lowering inpatient days, admissions, and average length of stay, all three in Illinois and Iowa, where most of their employees are; they are the largest employer in Iowa and one of the largest in Illinois. They are also active in Iowa, especially with the state legislature and the governor's office, in trying either to change laws that prevent innovative cost containment approaches or to enact provisions they think will help. Iowa just recently, under the prodding in part of a broader-based coalition, has passed a uniform data reporting act that will help provide a better data base for employers to use in riding herd on their utilization.

Our next speaker is Roger Wheeler of the Control Data Corporation, which is active in many areas of business initiative, including health care cost containment.

ROGER WHEELER, Control Data Corporation: There is a dilemma built into our topic that I would like to explore a bit: although we are talking about a national issue, the delivery mechanism is local. Therefore, the problem has a changing profile for any employer with more than one location. As a consequence, the powerful tool of plan design, which we probably have the most control over and can make the greatest community contribution through, is no longer a single mechanism but has to be a whole fabric of mechanisms.

At Control Data we have a $16 million bill for medical care. We have always had a single plan nationally. We have always required employee contributions, have never been in a first-dollar situation. Despite that, we face the subject that Ms. Schoen talked about—the cost shifting inside a plan to employees—and we have had to face how the kind of educated decision that employees must make and the resulting cost shift should take place.

First, we begin by changing the bias in our plan not just to an equal emphasis on inpatient and outpatient care but to a bias toward outpatient care—that is, a lesser deductible and smaller copayments for outpatient care.

Second, in the Twin Cities, where there are six active and healthy HMOs, for the last two years the HMOs have been less expensive than the insured approach. That is, the company's cost of insured care on the indemnity plan has been higher than the company's contribution could have been to an HMO; but federal law requires a contribution to HMOs equivalent to that for the indemnified approach. Our choice then was whether we should reexamine our whole reimbursement mechanism. We decided that, since there was no law on this subject, we could reimburse employees for their indemnified approach at the average reimbursement for HMOs. Effective January 1 last year we made that absolute reversal, which increased the contribution of employees who chose to remain in the indemnified plan but reduced the cost to employees who chose an HMO.

The next problem we faced was geographical differences. The competing HMOs in the Twin Cities do not exist almost anywhere else that Control Data has a large concentration of employees. We have 60 percent participation rates in HMOs in the Twin Cities and no more than 15 percent in any other location. For the first time in Control Data's history, we had to start shifting costs on the basis of geographical differences. That is, in some cities where there were less costly alternatives, we changed the reimbursement mixture between employees and the employer to encourage the lesser-cost alternatives.

We have a very active wellness program and, because we are both self-insured and self-administered, we have an excellent data base on hospital utilization and on the basis of participation in wellness programs. We have shown from three years' experience that smokers in our plan have claims 37 percent higher than nonsmokers. Fitness differences in the neighborhood of 20 to 25 percent are beginning to show themselves. We have a very significant difference in claims costs between employees who abuse drugs and other employees. The dilemma we face, therefore, is this: if employees choose not to participate in the wellness program and take the responsibility for managing that aspect of their lives, should other employees be expected to share the cost of their higher use of the system? Our philosophical decision so far is that they should not, and we are engaged in the architectural design of asking smokers who are unwilling to manage the problem, individuals unwilling to participate in fitness where there is a need, and people who are unwilling to accept treatment programs to accept an entirely different program of copayments and deductibles and start bearing a greater share of the burdens. That cost-shifting dilemma that we face I suspect many of you will face in your plans.

MR. SULLIVAN: Our last speaker is Bob Wilson. Although he is head of the Utah State Medical Association, he is here to speak as much for himself as a physician as for the medical association.

ROBERT G. WILSON, Utah State Medical Association: I do speak for myself and not for the physicians of Utah. I won't give you any new models, just a physician's perspective, so that you will understand the resistance you face and how I believe it must be overcome.

Peter Singer mentioned that when the Utah Health Cost Management Foundation tried to eliminate obstructions to preferred provider plans in the insurance code, the medical leadership was in favor of it, but the rank-and-file physicians simply came unglued when faced with competition. I heard very clearly up and down the state that they would rather work for a fixed fee than have to compete. That is a very alarming feeling I get from the medical community. I want you to understand that. We are asking doctors in midcareer to change their whole emphasis.

We have been taught in medical schools a chopped-liver approach to medical care. There is no particular wellness taught in departments of ophthalmology or obstetrics and gynecology or cardiovascular surgery. We are a procedure-oriented society. Not only are we taught procedures as physicians, but the media popularize them and patients and employees demand them. We have a difficulty with people who have been promised that when they graduate from a residency program, they will be paid to do these procedures. We must somehow reward the providers who are more efficient now; we must change them in midlife. The ivory tower and the way medicine is taught in this country should not be left out of the equation, and we must emphasize wellness.

This brings me to a word about payment and equity and the schizophrenia in medical practice today, which concerns the way we are paid. As a dermatologist, for instance, I may labor for quite a few minutes with a family with a significant skin eruption for $30, whereas it takes me two milliseconds to treat a precancerous lesion for the same price. Internists for years have said that it is worth just as much to take care of hypertension as to perform a procedure that takes half the time and is rewarded four times as well. Until we put the providers at some risk, we will not solve the problem; that is why, if the market approach is to succeed, the providers must be put at significant risk.

Group practice solves another difficulty. Is it worth $2,800 for an ophthalmologist to put in a lens implant? I do not think the public can decide that issue. The only way we can decide that issue is to put the money in the pot and let the individual providers decide what is appropriate. They will fight it out. The public is not ready to decide what is worth what.

Now there is a malpractice problem, whether it is real or apparent. I have badgered groups of physicians in the past year to provide me with some guidelines for appropriateness of care. I just got a very interesting letter from a group of emergency room physicians who listed PYA procedures. I read this whole three-page letter about PYA procedures, and I finally had to call the chief of the emergency room group and ask what a PYA procedure is. It is "protect your ass." So procedures are done to protect ourselves from either real or perceived malpractice problems. Clark Havighurst of Duke University has written an interesting paper that really frightened me, which made this point: not only is there a malpractice problem now, but in the writing of new group practice contracts, in attempts to ration care appropriately, in attempts to reduce delivery of medical care to what is appropriate, will contracts hold up when malpractice lawyers get wind of the fact that a plan has left out this or that service? This country simply has not dealt with that yet. I can ration medical care very effectively if someone will protect me. There is absolutely no need, for instance, to send every piece of tissue to the laboratory. David Eddy of Duke points out that the difference between one pap smear every year and one every two years is many millions of dollars but is only six days in the life of the average woman in this country. But who is willing to stand up and establish that as an appropriate guideline of care? We have not come to grips with how to ration care in an appropriate way.

One last comment: we in this country have not yet decided whether we consider medical care a right (that is, a need) or a privilege (that is, a commodity). If we adopt a market approach, it is a commodity to be bought and sold. I see a lot of problems with that; I believe the pendulum will someday swing back because we are not answering the needs of the most deserving—the poor and the ever-increasing elderly population in this country—and that does alarm me somewhat.

MR. SULLIVAN: I will open the floor now to comments and questions from the audience.

MIKE MAIBACH, Caterpillar Tractor Company: I have a question for Ms. Schoen. Many of us in this room believe that employees have to begin to feel the cost of health care. Our company has first-dollar coverage, and we need to change that; yet I cannot imagine a union supporting such a thing during a collective bargaining session. Can you respond to that matter?

MS. SCHOEN: I can respond in two ways. One, when I have taken a close look at many of our plans, I have found that most of them are not first dollar, at least not in the sense that the first time someone goes to a doctor everything is paid for. To the extent they are first dollar, the first dollar is for hospital costs and not for everything else. Patients pay substantially when they do not go to the hospital. So one of the things we have been supportive of is an expansion on the ambulatory side; along with prior authorization for admission and medical necessity on the need to go to the hospital, we have had a much bigger response in overall utilization and cost patterns than we would get with a copayer deductible. So we advocate doing those things first. We do not support higher deductibles and higher copayments.

I also do not think it necessary to look at the high-cost users of the plan. A small percentage of people are in the hospital for a long time because they are sick, they have an intense care need; you are not getting at that problem in any way with a $50 deductible. You buy grief when you come to the table saying that this year the deductible is going up. In some plans where we have had fairly good coverage on the hospital side, an exposure to $750 to $1,000 for hospital care just does not go anywhere. If you say you are genuinely interested in controlling overall costs, people perceive that as just meaning that they pay $1,000 before you start to pay anything.

JACK COFFEY, Rockford College: I have two questions about PPOs that anyone is welcome to answer. First, would someone elaborate on the antitrust and other legal problems of PPOs? Second, when offering a discounted service to employers with little or no payment by employees—and that is the incentive for employers to join a PPO—how do you avoid the problem of driving up the use of services by the employee and thereby in the long run increasing the cost for the employer?

CLARK HAVIGHURST, Duke University: I am no more prepared to give a definition of PPOs than anybody else, but perhaps it would be helpful in giving an answer to the antitrust question. A PPO may be organized by the providers themselves, hospitals and doctors. That would present the most serious antitrust problem. It could also be organized by an insurer that says it will cover a certain group of providers for certain services on a more favorable basis than other providers. The idea is to induce the insured to use the provider that has been shown to be either lower cost because it charges a lower price or more efficient because it uses the hospital less intensively.

As far as the antitrust issues are concerned, I have never thought the typical PPO ran much of a risk. The Supreme Court last year decided a case involving a foundation for medical care in Arizona, which had set itself up to establish maximum fees that doctors could charge; the Court said that was price fixing. A PPO could be seen as an organization of providers who had agreed on a fee or agreed to accept no more than a certain price, and it is that seeming parallel that leads to the concern that there is an antitrust violation. The difference is that PPOs are typically not as powerful in the marketplace as that foundation was in Arizona. There the organization was set up by the medical society and essentially represented all the fee-for-service physicians in the state or in the counties involved. In one county at least 70 percent of the doctors participated. A typical PPO would not involve nearly as high a percentage of physicians or hospitals. We do not know the exact percentage at which the risk disappears, although we could get some sense of that from some Federal Trade Commission (FTC) work. At any rate, the problem exists only if the PPO represents a large percentage; certainly if it represents more than half, there would be a concern, but if it were less than that, there should not be much concern. A speech by Walter Winslow, assistant deputy director of the Bureau of Competition of the FTC, addressed this issue in some detail recently; it is a very thoughtful statement of the FTC's view about which PPOs are lawful and which are not.

MR. SULLIVAN: Would anybody here like to comment on the second part of the question?

MR. KLEIN: I have an additional comment on the antitrust considerations. I am not an attorney, and so you have to qualify my remarks in that regard. There are two varieties of PPOs. One is that already described, which is organized and offered by a group of doctors and hospitals, where there is a different set of antitrust concerns. The second type is organized by an insurance company or a Blue Cross–Blue Shield plan, there being no provider organization but merely a contract between hospitals and doctors and the insurance carrier, and in this the notion of price fixing does not enter. There are other problems with insurance carriers or Blue Cross plans setting up a preferred provider product, problems related to the questions of freedom of choice and discrimination. You have to be careful how you select your panel. You have to provide fairly equal opportunity for all, at least so our attorneys have told us. Our preferred provider products have addressed the issue of utilization control in a variety of ways, some through economic incentives, some through actual use control procedures. In Minnesota we established fourteen categories—a diagnostic related group (DRG) system with fourteen groups rather than 467—with a target for length of stay and a per diem based on the case mix for each contracting hospital; so economically we have some control there. We still may have some excess admissions, but as we develop that program further—and we are looking toward paying some sort of bonus to physicians for reduced admission rates—we should be able to get a control there as well. In some of the other areas where there have been use control procedures, typically we will write into the contract with the hospital or the doctor requirements for fairly stringent preadmission certification or concurrent review rules, those rules to be administered by a medical association, a PSRO, or by the Blue Cross–Blue Shield plan itself.

MR. HAVIGHURST: As David Greenberg points out in his health law digest from the National Health Lawyers Association, a recent FTC advisory opinion indicated that a certain PPO in California was lawful, and that might be another reference to follow up. On Mr. Klein's point about having to be careful in selecting the members of the PPO, I agree that lawyers will tell you to be careful, but I think a better reading of antitrust laws is that you can choose anybody you want on any basis you want. It makes a whole lot more sense for private entities, even big ones like Blue Cross and Blue Shield, to be free to be selective. That is how competition works, buyers deciding from whom they want to buy, sellers deciding with whom they want to do business. Antitrust has frequently gotten confused on this point. It is useful to start from the proposition that any organization wanting to compete in the marketplace is free to be selective. If you get involved in litigation, you should realize that you are fighting to establish a principle that is worthwhile.

MR. SINGER: I would like to elaborate on the legal obstacle to development of PPOs in Utah. This law apparently exists in various forms in fifteen to twenty other states; so I encourage you to take a close look at your own state's statutes. In Utah in the early 1970s, the chiropractors and the psychologists and the podiatrists were not covered by a number of insurance carriers. Obviously they did not like that; so they passed a law known as the antidiscrimination section, which says that no insurer may offer a policy in Utah that in any way restricts the full freedom of choice of the insured to choose any licensed provider. Most legal counsel has indicated that a 100 percent versus an 80 percent benefit differential in a preferred provider plan would definitely be construed as restriction of full freedom of choice. There is now a bill in Congress sponsored by Representative Ron Wyden of Oregon that would preempt all such state obstacles to PPO development.

MR. GOLDBECK: I would like to speak more to the second half of the question. In any kind of negotiated provider arrangement, employers need data upon which to base their negotiating position. To find out that they pay a hospital x and to negotiate for 10 percent less means absolutely nothing. Any intelligent hospital administrator could manage to get that 10 percent back very quickly, and any insurance carrier or third-party administrator who negotiates a little discount is just playing games. It doesn't do you a nickel's worth of good in the long run. You need data that show you—by procedure, with national codes—where your problem is. Then you can negotiate volume arrangements, changes in practice patterns, changes in utilization patterns, cooperative agreements among provider organizations, and so on, and you can begin to package the system and guide people to the appropriate providers for the appropriate services. You can then realize a benefit with or without a discount because you are changing behavior. The purpose of the preferred provider arrangement is to change behavior; the changes in dollars follow. Without the changes in behavior, it is just a shell game. You want to move people through a system, not just get a discount for the people already in the system and let the system continue to do the same garbage, and there is no point in getting 10 percent less than something that is no good to begin with. You want 10 percent less than a better something, something that really will benefit you in the long run through changes in practice patterns.

The question implied that employees who go into a preferred arrangement have to go in with 100 percent coverage. That is also not correct. It can be 80 percent to go to the preferred plan, 50 percent or 20 percent to go to the nonpreferred plan, or any other combination of numbers. There are no rules; it is whatever incentives you can best figure out.

The important thing to recognize is that PPOs are being characterized as operating by freedom of choice, where employers and unions will negotiate great deals and tell the employees to use the plan if they want to. Some of America's failing businesses and unions may take that posture for a while but not many of them. If they really get a good deal, they are going to negotiate their employees into it. The whole purpose of a negotiated plan is to get somebody to use it, not to have it as something to talk about at a meeting. There may never be a rule that says thou shalt go to this doctor or this hospital, but the economic incentives are going to be so clear that unless someone has a medical reason why he cannot go there, that is where he is going to go. The more successful the negotiation, the more there is an incentive to get people into that plan.

My last point is that no matter what provider arrangement you negotiate as an employer, there is no way to avoid having to help manage the system. If you sign a contract and think you don't have to worry about it for the next three years, you are going to get cheated by that deal just as you do in any other deal because that is the nature of the game. The underlying message is that you have to manage the system, and the payer, not the surrogates for the payer, has to be involved in the management process.

MR. ARNOULD: The PPO concept initially covered mainly those things that involved direct negotiation by employers for health care services. There were two or three reasons for that, one of which was to guarantee a direct purchase arrangement at a fixed price. Another was to bypass the insurer. The health insurance industry has not been innovative, and now we often call almost everything that comes along in the way of a new or an alternative payment system a PPO. That may be all right, but let's separate out the one thing that was intended in the beginning.

If I look at the way the insurance industry has acted in the past, I am a little concerned about being in a room with the lion that bit me last year. What are their incentives? Is the insurance industry going to police these arrangements, or is it back in your laps either to let it go as in the past or to provide your own policing? I think you need to provide your own policing mechanism to get the necessary utilization review and control.

MR. DEDMON: I have another question that relates to the insurance industry that I would like to couch in a positive way. With all the changing governmental controls, with DRGs and all that sort of thing, what steps is the insurance industry taking to provide those of us in industry who are concerned about costs with information that we can understand—what was done to whom, where, when, by whom, and to what age, sex, race, or type of employee does this individual belong? My superficial experience is that we cannot understand the information we get. We have to hire an outside consultant to tell us what it means. Simplifying the data we receive from the insurance people would be a great step toward getting some of the data we need.

BARBARA WARDEN, National Consumers League: I have a question directed to David Klein of Chicago Blue Cross–Blue Shield, which is in part a follow-up to the comments just made. There has been an excellent discussion this morning about utilization of services and controlling costs. One of the problems from the consumer's point of view is the padding of bills. David Klein mentioned in his laundry list a bill-monitoring project of Blue Cross. I am curious to know just what kind of bill-monitoring project it is. Is it possible not only for employers to receive bills that are easy to understand and do not require an outside consultant to translate, but also for consumers? Consumers are being charged for services they did not receive, and yet they are at a loss to know how to challenge or analyze the bill. I would be interested to know if your bill-monitoring project addresses that problem.

MR. KLEIN: The bill audit has been in place in some Blue Cross plans for many years; in others it is of more recent vintage. In some cases, it is tied to a fraudulent abuse program; in others it operates independently. We customize what we do to the needs of each community. The process is typically on a sample basis. We go with our claims to the hospital, pull medical records, and check whether the services shown on the claims have in fact been delivered. If they have not, we make an adjustment on that particular bill. If it appears to be a pervasive situation, where the error rate is 5, 10, or 15 percent, some negotiation takes place with the hospital to reduce our overall payment. That reduction is passed back either in future adjustments to our accounts or in retroactive adjustments, depending on the nature of our contract. There are situations in which we have tried to explain better what services have been provided, but they have not progressed at the same rate. We could do more work in that area.

MS. WARDEN: One other quick follow-up question—do you have any procedure for handling consumer complaints at any of the local Blue Cross–Blue Shield offices that would permit an individual consumer who had insurance coverage to challenge the charges on a bill?

MR. KLEIN: Again, that varies; in some locations we have that, but it is not a universal program. If the consumer had this problem and it was called to our attention in the absence of a formal procedure, I am sure we would deal with it.

ALEXANDER KOVACS, Medical Society of New Jersey: Health care is divided into various parts, of which medical care is only 8 percent. Hospitalization constitutes about 60 percent; nursing care, dental care, drugs, nursing home care, eyeglasses, and so forth make up the rest. Now we have a search for the factors responsible for the cost increases, and this immediately leads to three principal parties that determine the cost and the prices—the American people, who demand health care services, the medical industry that provides these services, and the political apparatus of the government that regulates and manipulates both.

Regulation has not been touched on by any of the panelists here. The health care industry is cast as the inflator attempting to raise the prices and the government as the great stabilizer fighting to constrain the cost and the prices. In reality, government regulations are making ever more expensive demands on the health industry, which reduce the quantity and the quality of services and increase the cost. Cost containment is not solely a patient's decision; a patient expects the highest quality of care. Neither is cost containment solely the hospital's prerogative. Energy costs, increasing charges for supplies and drugs, general inflation, rules and regulations, and salaries and benefits are contributing to the costs, and the hospitals are caught in the middle.

If cost containment is the objective for future health care, we must determine how decisions should be made and by whom. Decisions should be made on the basis of needs. We must separate what is necessary from what we would like to have. Rationing, which is what will happen with the PPOs and the HMOs, will shortly be on us, and it should be based on economics, but based as well on what the public perceives as necessary and not what some individual or group thinks all of society should have, and politics should not be a part of the decision. We have not touched on government regulations and how they are increasing the cost of care. Could somebody comment on that?

MR. ARNOULD: There is no question that regulation has cost implications. Some regulations hit the health care industry just as they do industry generally: equal employment, various safety codes, and so on. Those are not costs that the health care industry can speak to as though they were unique to it. Other kinds of state and local regulation are perceived as onerous by various elements of the industry and as entirely beneficial by other elements. One can characterize regulation as being supported by those for whom it produces a market advantage and generally opposed by those for whom it does not. There is nothing unique about this industry in that regard.

When we talk about the role of government, particularly what it has done to costs with the Medicare and Medicaid programs, we should not lose sight of one thing. The government lost an opportunity in 1965 to create an innovative health care system. It might have worked, or it might have been a disaster; we don't know, but the opportunity was lost. What the government did in 1965 was to duplicate all the bad parts of the private sector's system as political tradeoffs to gain the support of the various leading hospital and medical insurance constituencies. That was the reality. It is not as though somebody had conjured up a governmental program that was pernicious and had all these terrible elements and was unique and innovative and just failed. It simply copied what was already failing and has failed right along with the private elements for the remaining nineteen years now. We really should not be surprised.

DR. WILSON: To answer the consumer advocate, Barbara Warden—PSROs showed that if we go after the tail of the bell-shaped curve and try to get the people who pad a few bills and the bad guys, we will spend an enormous amount of money saving a few dollars. We have to take the whole mass of the bell-shaped curve and move it to the efficient side. We can go after those people, hire the smartest lawyer, and still cannot put them out of business.

MR. ARNOULD: Two or three of us here started our talks by apologizing because we are in a session on new models and cost containment and yet are still talking about HMOs and PPOs, which we have heard about for five to ten years.

There are very few communities where as much as 20 percent of the population has ever been part of an HMO and fewer who have ever been involved in a PPO or in the utilization review programs being developed by corporations. We have to start doing because we are not going to learn which of these are best just by philosophizing about them. That is what I am supposed to do because I am the academic economist, but I have no data to study until you people do some things to start showing us what part of this menu is going to work and what part will have to be dropped.

DR. WILSON: I want to stress one thing that has been mentioned—appropriate rationing. The business sector must take part in that. It concerns me that when someone is sick, we cannot ration care; we cannot make rational decisions at the eleventh hour. I was excited to hear that corporations are beginning to make such ethical choices as even to think about charging the smoker more than the nonsmoker. That is the most significant thing that has been said here today.

MR. HAVIGHURST: I want to pick up on a theme I heard several times, first from Mr. Wardrop and then from Ms. Schoen and then from Bill Goldbeck. The idea was that we should not try to drive a hard bargain with a hospital to get a lower price. That bothers me because I would have thought that to be the first order of business, what a capitalist would do. I thought we were dealing with capitalists here, and it turns out we are dealing with socialists or others who think we must be concerned about the whole society, the whole system. Driving hard bargains with a hospital may be a good way of getting the ball rolling because—if it does shift costs to others who are paying higher prices—maybe they will find a way to drive a hard bargain. When driving hard bargains proliferates throughout a community, there is suddenly a very cost-conscious and competitive system going. Although that is not all that needs to be done by any means—a lot of systemization and management and other things must be put in—driving hard bargains is a good place to start.

MR. GOLDBECK: I would have to admit to a certain pleasure in being attacked for not being a capitalist in this setting, but I am not against driving hard bargains; I think that is fine. I trust the record of the last several years would support that. My point is that a major corporation can negotiate a 20 percent discount with any hospital in town; if it does that without knowing that 20 percent is off hospital charges that can be 200, 300, 400, or 500 percent higher per procedure than those of the hospital across the street, it is negotiating hard out of ignorance. It must develop the data base so that when it comes to the table to negotiate, it comes with the armament of information that enables it to drive a hard bargain in the best setting.

COMMENT: A situation could arise where some company bargains very hard and gets a less-than-market price for its share and thus drives out competitors from that market. If I am not concerned about what happens in the rest of the system but only concerned about myself and drive a very good hard bargain, of course I would love that because I would end up with 100 percent or 95 percent of the market. We should not take this concept of bargaining to the extreme; we have situations currently where people say they have an advantage in the marketplace because they have bargained hard and in fact they have 85 percent of the market.

MR. SULLIVAN: I will ask Dick Wardrop to wrap this up with a few final remarks.

MR. WARDROP: I am not sure I should have agreed to do a summary of this. It is like wrapping a jellyfish as a gift. I am not sure we invented any new models, but we did establish some things that may be helpful.

First, I think I can conclude that the private sector initiatives are better focused and stronger than they have been in the past. Second, malpractice insurance is a real problem. It is also used as a copout by some of the medical community, but it is a real problem that the private sector should not ignore. Third, health insurance as we have known it is vanishing. When we hear that we are going to charge the sick more and give refunds to the healthy, that is no longer insurance; it is counter to the principle of insurance. I am not judging whether it is right or wrong. We are going to segment the market by charging the sick more and giving money back to the healthy, and there is a trend in that direction. Fourth, the private sector looks at health care costs as at any other expense. There is no difference between that expense and any other service or product. The private sector has finally come to that realization. Therefore we need to develop strategies to deal with it, and one of the ways to deal with it is locally.

There is now a broad-based coalition in Pittsburgh, for example, with nine cosponsors, including the United Steelworkers of America, the Urban League, the Hospital Council, the Medical Society, the

Pittsburgh Business Group on Health, and the Allegheny Conference on Community Development. It has a three-phased program: to reduce inpatient hospitalization by 10 percent, to take 10 percent of the medical-surgical beds out of service, and to establish an overall decrease in health care expenses for the community. So a broad-based community has decided on that as a project.

Finally, a system change is necessary through some kind of alternative delivery system.

Shifting the Cost of Health Care: Private Sector Response, Public Policy Reforms

MR. ESCH: As we move into this afternoon's session we hope you will be willing not only to present items on your own agenda but to respond to the other panelists, so that we can begin to crystallize some of the differences and interests among us.

We would like to have two persons frame the discussion before we move into a more aggressive crossfertilization of ideas. We have asked Larry Lewin, president of Lewin and Associates, to begin our afternoon's discussion. Lewin and Associates perhaps more than any other group is looking at private sector involvement and what is going on in the field in a very significant way.

LAWRENCE LEWIN, Lewin and Associates: If I had to put a title on what I am going to talk about, it would be "Cost Shifting—Villain or Scapegoat?" I am more inclined toward the latter view, that it is more a scapegoat than a villain.

It is probably becoming clear to everyone that we are entering or are well into the era of the purchaser. For years we talked about reform of the health care system and about trying to change the reimbursement system to bring about systemwide reform. That has really become a thing of the past. Even though some of the strategies of today may arguably be in support of system reform, it is clear that we are in an era where it is every person for himself or herself. Nowhere is that more apparent than in the position taken by the federal government as symbolized in the approach to the Medicare reimbursement program for hospitals. One could argue, of course, if one is cynical enough, that the whole animus is really to reduce the fiscal liability, but I think a strong case could be made that each purchaser must do his best to lower costs. The aggregate effect might be a better, more efficient system. There are some other consequences of the era of the purchaser that Mr. Wardrop referred to at the beginning, such as the erosion of the traditional concept of insurance pools in the health care system. We will still end up with insurance, but it will look different.

The best characterization of what the era of the purchaser means is a story about two fellows who were camping in Glacier National Forest. In the middle of the night one woke up and saw a grizzly bear coming up the road toward his tent. When he started to put on his running shoes, his friend asked, "What are you doing?" "I'm putting on my running shoes." "Why are you doing that? You can't outrun a grizzly bear." "I don't have to outrun the grizzly bear; I only have to outrun you." If we face up to it honestly, that is a direct implication of the era of the purchaser. There are going to be some losers; some of us are going to end up better than the rest. As we get into this game, the most obvious aggressive player seems to be the Medicare program, but it is clear that what is being urged is that we all get into the game that way.

In looking at cost shifting, we need to break it apart into some of its pieces to deal with it more effectively. There are two basic breaks. The first is that part of cost shifting that has to do with whether or not each payer is going to bear his or her fair share of costs, and that includes costs of research, teaching, bad debts, and charity care. The second major piece is to understand that a lot of what is called cost shifting is the result of some purchasers' seeking a reasonable price to pay per unit of output. We can think of Medicare paying a price for a DRG defined admission as an effort not just to reduce liability, to try to pay below costs, but to define what are reasonable costs by some measure. We can argue whether that system produces reasonable costs, but it is important to distinguish between those two types of cost shifting.

On the fair share notion, government is considered the great culprit. I would not include Blue Cross as a culprit because by and large Blue Cross picks up some share of bad debt and teaching costs, but we tend to think of government as the great culprit. That is a point that Jack Meyer makes in his pamphlet on Medicare and Medicaid.

Medicare certainly does not pay all costs. It takes the position that a portion of teaching costs will be covered but certain research costs will not be, in part because there is a National Institutes of Health (NIH) program. The argument is, in fact, that we gave at the office; we have already supported major efforts of research as a government and therefore should not be part of the system. Those are arguable points, but there are some merits on both sides. Probably the place where the Medicare program is most vulnerable is in the failure to pay its share of bad debts. The argument is that there are no bad debts for the population that it covers, but of course that leads us into the Catch-22 that the only people who will pay for bad debts are those who don't pay their bills. In New York and Massachusetts, where there is now an effort to define all-payer systems, the Medicare programs are now paying some share of bad debt and charity costs. The real burden for failing to pay a fair share falls on the states, in part because Medicaid programs in many states are not paying cost-based rates but discounts; even though the federal government is willing to pay a share of costs, it is ultimately the state's decision what the reimbursement system will look like. Second, and very important, the states are the ones who are responsible for those poor and underinsured who are not in the Medicaid program, and this constitutes a fairly significant share of the cost-shifting burden, that is, the bad debt and particularly the charity cases. Our experience is that this group is growing and becoming a more serious burden—both on private payers and on state governments.

It is worth noting from the standpoint of the corporate purchaser, the major private employer, what some of the distributive effects of these policies are. Corporate taxes constitute about 6 percent of total state revenues, and corporations contribute about 25 percent of total private health insurance premiums. What does that mean? If government payments to hospitals are reduced and corporate tax bills thereby lowered, and those costs are shifted to the private payer with the leverage that cost shifting implies—that is, if the private payers end up paying a bigger share of the cost-shifted burden—it is a poor bargain from the viewpoint of a taxpaying corporation. There is a lot of leverage in the distributive effect. That suggests that it is economically valid for the private purchaser and the private purchasing community to get very interested in and vocal about the way states finance or fail to finance care for the poor. Clearly what happened in Massachusetts and New York is a byproduct of that concern. State legislators need to be helped to become better informed about the fact that there is no way to hide these costs. There is no free lunch; somebody is paying for it, and some of the distributions are very inequitable.

My experience in dealing with state legislators on the issue of the medically indigent is that they tend not to be well informed. There are many options, most of them with different implications for who should pay: expanding Medicaid to the medically needy, direct financing of the medically indigent, catastrophic insurance, mandating of coverage for small employers, assigning risk pools, or direct support for public general hospitals. All of these are options. It would behoove the private purchaser to get involved politically in these questions.

The second part of this issue is reasonable price, and the point here is very simple. If the purpose of Medicare or other so-called prudent purchasers is to reduce the cost to themselves and thus bring about change in the system, this will happen only if providers of care have nowhere else to shift that cost. That seems obvious. What is always surprising to me is that discussions of cost shifting rarely focus on the role of the provider but focus on the role of the purchaser. The purchaser is left with a couple of choices. One is to seek help from government, to resist the cost shift by establishing all-payer reimbursement systems. It is ironic that this antiregulatory administration through its Medicare reimbursement policies is stimulating cost shifting that has had the direct effect of having businesses give major support to the all-payer system, as in Massachusetts.

Clearly the effect in many states among employers who feel they are going to be subjected to a flood of cost-shifted dollars is to seek an all-payer system or, as Jack Meyer prefers to call it, mandated rate setting. Some very well-informed people feel it is not a bad idea, but it should be pointed out that an all-payer system need not be a fixed rate. It could be a maximum rate. Many all-payer systems preclude the kind of negotiation that we were talking about this morning; in their early stages DRGs in New Jersey prevented HMOs from making their own deals, which was a real flaw. That has now been corrected.

There is another option, and that is to fight back. Some of our research suggests the importance of local leadership; that leadership can take the form of organizing and providing direction to coalitions (I would just add that many coalitions merely take the form of everybody sitting around the table). I favor those coalitions that offer an unadulterated forum for purchasers, for employers, to get together and express their point of view and be heard. Another form local leadership can take is to find some way to communicate the notion that patients will be shifted from one provider to another on the basis of economic circumstances. We are seeing a dramatic interest in PPOs in California and also in south Florida, two very different communities. The one characteristic both of them face is that providers are getting the message that patients may be moved to the most efficient provider. Corporate leadership must take enough interest in this issue to make it clear that that bullet will be bitten. That may be more important than picking a particular mechanism for doing it.

All the particulars are important. Data are critical; without appropriate, claims-oriented data, there will not be a basis for making PPO decisions. The first round of data collection was related to gross hospital statistics, and that is not enough. We need claims data, and we may need support from government to get them, as Indiana and Iowa have done. The opposition the providers will put up as rearguard action is indicative of how important they think this is. Uses must be found for those data, including utilization review. Support for alternative systems is another way to communicate that patients will be moved, that options will be put in place. As the hospitals move into the latter part of the 1980s, their greatest concern will be control and stability of their market share. Many hospitals can operate with a smaller volume provided that their market share is relatively stable. The kind of moving around of patients that is possible now increasingly tends to threaten this and therefore becomes a strong negotiating leverage.

Let me close with two brief points. First, it is important not to rely on government to bail us out and solve the problems for us, but we should not ignore the important role of government, nor should we ignore the opportunity to seek partnerships, whether it be in defining better medically indigent financing techniques or helping us to get promarket reforms like better data. The second point is that we have to be impressed by the enormously rapid changes that are taking place. We are looking at models that we could not have imagined five years ago, and I suspect that what we will be talking about here five years from now will be even more exciting and more innovative than anything we can imagine today.

MR. ESCH: We have heard an overview of what might happen in the private sector. To give us a bridge to the public sector, we turn to our host for the day, Jack Meyer.

DR. MEYER: I see the problem of cost shifting as a symptom of a much larger problem in American society and in government. We can look at health care and acknowledge that as patients we want it all, but perhaps we do not want to pay for wanting it all. Our desires as users of a system may outrun our wallets and our willingness to ante up. Is that really different from us as veterans, as civil servants, as farmers, as pensioners, as all those who rely on the federal government in one form or another for assistance? Their collective desires may outrun the collective body politic's willingness as taxpayers to finance them. It is clear there was a mandate to bring more fiscal austerity to our federal budget. I want to suggest that, despite all the austerity in recent years, we have yet to face up to this paradox and the tension between our promises and the resources we are willing to make available to meet those promises.

A major problem has been the way we have shared the austerity. There are those who would disagree even with the need for it, but I do not want to raise macroeconomic policy issues. I want to examine for a moment the sharing of the burden. In some recent work I have been doing, I have found that a very disproportionate share of the burden has fallen on those people who depend on government programs for low-income families. We went through much of the last couple of years largely exempting what I would call the battleships and destroyers in the federal armada, which were increasingly headed into troubled financial waters. We have been through this in social security; some would say we still are not out of troubled waters. Medicare is next. The budget cuts that were made hardly touched in the first year and only began to touch in the second year programs like old age and survivors' insurance, Medicare, civil service retirement—a real ticking time bomb—veterans, and so on. Proportionately the government rather sharply cut the benefits going to our lowest-income citizens, particularly those who are not dependent poor, the so-called near poor and working poor, who were largely stripped of all aid from the federal government. I made an attempt to aggregate those social programs that are not means tested and found surprisingly that the share of the federal budget they accounted for in 1980 is almost identical with the share projected for them under the most recent Reagan budget for 1988. That is, after eight years of a pretty tough austerity program, regardless of what other cuts we might make, that share—a little over 40 percent—will not have changed at all.

By contrast, the share going to low-income programs, means-tested programs, which of course are smaller, has fallen from about 13.3 percent in 1980; it is headed down to 9 percent under current policies in 1988. That is a cut of about a third in the share of federal dollars going to those programs. I raise this not to get off on budget issues but because I think that the health care sector is a kind of microcosm of the fairness issue and that if we do not come up with a more evenhanded approach—both in health care and more broadly in government policy—which begins to take a little bit from all, mainly on the basis of who can afford to sacrifice the most, instead of disproportionately from those who can afford it the least, we will see a hue and cry for a return to overpromising, a mentality that got us into so much difficulty with our constituents in the first place. So I am groping for a sustainable set of policies that can move us to a better alternative.

In health care the largest federal program of course is Medicare, with some $60 billion in projected outlays in the coming fiscal year. The second largest program is not Medicaid; it is the tax subsidy associated with the full exclusion from employees' taxable income of employers' contributions to health insurance. This subsidy has been estimated by two of our conference participants today—Gail Wilensky and Amy Taylor—at about $31 billion for 1983, half again as large as the federal contribution to Medicaid, which is now about $20 billion. Yet what have we been cutting most in the last two or three years?—Medicaid. We haven't touched the tax subsidy; we haven't until very recently touched Medicare.

Now that is beginning to change, and as the fairness issue becomes more widespread, we will see more and more of an attempt to get a handle on the big battleships, to make midcourse changes in their course. And this will bring the cost-shifting issue to the fore. In other words, we ain't seen nothing yet, as the federal government grapples with bringing its promises to our elderly in line with our resources. The share of the elderly in the federal budget has gone up by one percentage point since 1980, from 26 to 27 percent, according to a recent study. I do not raise the tax subsidy cap here to lobby for it; it can be debated in other forums whether it is good or bad health policy. I bring it up in the context of fairness. How fair is it that we are unwilling to nick at the margin the employee whose employer contributes $300 a month to a very generous first-dollar-for-everything-coverage insurance plan but are willing to make major nicks in those getting Medicaid—and that many people who are poor or near poor are still ineligible for any government help? That is the question we need to resolve.

I favor an incentives-based approach to enhancing the efficiency and equity of the health care system. But I favor these reforms, like a tax subsidy ceiling, like vouchers for Medicare, because I think they are fair and will give us more for our dollar. They will not resolve the financial crisis in Medicare by themselves; they will not resolve the dilemma we face because of our unwillingness to pay up and our ever-present desire to hide the costs through efforts like cost shifting. I think my reforms will help more, and others think theirs will help more in reducing the gap. We can debate that, and careful evaluations by groups like Lewin and Associates will give us evidence on which approaches and innovations work best, but we are left with the sober realization that neither DRGs nor rate setting nor for that matter market reforms will fully resolve this problem. Given the demographic situation we face, given the technological explosions that we face, the problem will be exacerbated. That is another aspect of the fact that we ain't seen nothing yet.

The Congressional Budget Office has recently estimated that Medicare will be some $300 billion in deficit by 1994. The recent report of the trustees of the Social Security Commission indicates that 1990 or 1991 will be the point when it goes into the red. It is in deep trouble now. What will it be in as we continue to discover new devices like artificial hearts that we never even thought of before?

I raise these questions because I think we need to recognize that we are an undertaxed society in relation to the commitments we have made. That is not a plea for tax increases, although I predict that the next president of the United States, be he a Democrat or a Republican, will advocate a consumption tax because of this problem. I hope we will not just go back to raising marginal tax rates again, and maybe the government will prefer to trim benefits and raise taxes less. But we have to come up with some combination of what is euphemistically called revenue enhancement and what is less euphemistically called cutting benefits to the haves in our society so that there is more for the have-nots.

MR. ESCH: As one who has been in the political arena, I have been listening to all these comments about what we have done to ourselves in the private and public sector in this field in the last decade or decade and a half, and the difficulty we face now is one of limited resources, which we finally admit that we have. We didn't admit that a decade ago. In my generation, we thought we had unlimited resources, but now we admit we have limited resources and unlimited promises and we do not control the costs in either the public or the private sector. As an old politician, I would say that cost shifting is a political solution to an economic and social problem.

BERNARD R. TRESNOWSKI, Blue Cross and Blue Shield: The debate over cost shifting centers on three questions—whether it exists, what its dimensions are, and what to do about it. Those who assert that cost shifting exists and is of substantial magnitude move immediately to the conclusion that it is inherently bad and needs to be corrected through fundamental reforms in the payment system. The most popular suggestions include a federally mandated all-payer system and state rate regulation.

It is our belief that cost shifting is misunderstood, is not inherently bad, and does not require radical reform in the payment system. First, hospital net revenues do not equal costs. They include an operating margin, and each payer as a prudent buyer should negotiate its contribution. Just because over the bargaining table someone wants a 20 percent net margin, I do not necessarily have to give it to him. Bad debts and charity allowances are not costs but reductions in revenue. Again, each payer should negotiate a fair contribution to bad debts and charity. Medicare and Medicaid pay for their beneficiaries and thus reduce the bad debt and charity allowance of hospitals. One can argue that the very existence of Medicare and Medicaid is a contribution to bad debts and charity. Indeed, the extension of Medicare coverage to those with end stage renal disease is a further contribution to that reduction and to revenue. It should come as no surprise because it was quite clear when the law was enacted in 1965—we always called it "the young folks won't pay for the old folks" and vice versa. Moreover, provider costs vary by the characteristics of the beneficiaries and subscribers of the various payers and by the business practices of the various payers, and those payers should have the right to negotiate the real costs of providing care to their patients. Indeed there is a cost shift; certainly in the Medicare program the application of the limits established by the Tax Equity and Fiscal Responsibility Act of 1982 (TEFRA) will precipitate that if it hasn't already, and price limitations under the DRG system will also precipitate it, but they were designed to do that. They were designed in the context of incentives. The hospital has essentially three ways to deal with that. It can shift the costs, it can take the difference in its operating margin, or it can increase its productivity. We all hope that it would do the last.

A second belief is that cost shifting is not inherently bad. It is not inherently bad if it reflects differences in price based on negotiation. Our economy is based on the fact that all suppliers of goods and services provide unique prices to special buyers. It is not inherently bad if it is used in a way to recognize fairness and payment considering the contributions to net revenues of each payer, and it is not inherently bad if it is a way for hospitals to pay for the care of those otherwise unable to pay.

The third belief is that cost shifting does not require radical reform in the payment system. Federally mandated all-payer systems and state rate regulation are drastic answers to an issue that should be left at the bargaining table. Clearly, a payment system has more important things to do than to focus on the subject of cost shifting. It should concern itself with constraining costs but be designed to generate payments adequate to ensure the availability of needed services. Our experience also tells us that the results of the system depend more on its design and implementation than on the method itself. We believe that the payment system should influence utilization and capital investment decisions to ensure a positive effect on costs. These are the criteria and the characteristics of a payment system. Our conclusion is that no single best payment system exists given the regional variation and community needs and resources. Thus we see in Blue Cross and Blue Shield good results in Rhode Island, Massachusetts, Michigan, Rochester, New York—all under substantially different payment systems.

Under any of a variety of systems that fall within the general category of price-based competitive systems or regulatory systems, a responsible purchaser must seek fair prices for goods and services through a process of negotiation. In a negotiation process, neither party unilaterally sets the prices, nor does any outside party. Negotiating parties usually have conflicting interests and objectives, but the negotiation process is a strong and proven mechanism for balancing interests and devising acceptable compromises. It attempts to balance the responsibility of a carrier to pay only a fair price for services received by subscribers or beneficiaries against the hospital's responsibility to obtain fair payment for those services. Clearly, different carriers bring different strengths to health care financing. To the extent that some carriers pay slowly, provide sparse coverage, fail to cover poor risks, are inattentive to questionable utilization, or are ineffective in other ways, the cost of providing care to their customers will be higher than it needs to be. It is no more unusual for hospital prices to vary among payers than it is for interest rates or other contract prices to differ among businesses with differing financial characteristics. There should be a price differential between a payer that accepts hospital charges and a payer that effectively negotiates hospital payment based on the actual costs of serving subscribers or beneficiaries. Negotiations between a hospital and a carrier are sound business, and prudent purchase of service on behalf of subscribers should result in prices that differ from those the hospital expects other less effective and efficient carriers to pay.

In conclusion, I urge that we redirect our attention away from an issue that is misunderstood and not inherently bad and instead focus our imagination and our energies on how to provide the American people with access to high-quality health care at an affordable price. In the process of doing that, we should guard against throwing out the baby with the bathwater. Twenty years ago we set in motion a series of powerful incentives to give the American people access to increasingly sophisticated medical care, and we were not unmindful of the cost of achieving that objective. In 1968, at the request of President Johnson, John Gardner, then secretary of the Department of Health, Education, and Welfare, convened a high-level conference on health care costs, at which the important thinkers and policy makers of that time presented their views on how to control costs. The recommendations ranged from regulatory to competitive schemes, with many suggestions to redirect the incentives of the system. Most of those recommendations were turned into actions, including HMOs, health planning, utilization controls, payment systems, and others. They all had a positive effect, but they were insufficient to overcome the powerful forces of increased medical technology and the aging of the population. The problem today is more complex; it is fundamentally one of rationing a more technologically sophisticated health care product. This is not a simple problem subject to a simple solution. Bioethical questions are raised as well as questions of economics and affordability, but these are the problems that demand our attention, and they are the ones that will command it.

MICHAEL BROMBERG, Federation of American Hospitals: With respect to cost shifting, which is nothing more than cross-subsidization, I would like to make two points. One is that we would not have a cost-shifting problem if we had no revenue shortfall: if the federal government or some other government were willing to spend as much money as needed to take care of the poor and everyone else, there would not have to be a shift, and we would not be talking about it. What we are really talking about is a revenue problem, not a cost-shift question.

Second, cost shifting or cross-subsidization goes on throughout our economy but in a different way. Throughout the economy of this country, one purchaser pays less than another purchaser for various reasons, normally having to do with volume, sometimes having to do with government versus private sector purchasing. When someone buys a fleet of cars for his business, he gets a discount, and when someone else buys one car, part of the price he pays is subsidizing the discount given to the big-volume purchaser. We do not question this system in other parts of the economy, but we question it in health care, and we probably should, for one very good reason: the basic difference between health care and cars or airplanes that a manufacturer sells to the Pentagon for one price and to an airline for another is that in health care we have a tax subsidy that we do not have anywhere else. In effect, the taxpayers are subsidizing that cost shift through the tax subsidy.

I recommend to everyone a book that I have read about five times, Morris Abram's volume *Securing Access to Health Care*, a report prepared by the President's Commission for the Study of Ethical Problems in Medicine and Biomedical and Behavioral Research, chaired by Morris Abram. He writes of fairness and equity, and he raises some basic points. The first is that the $30 or $31 billion tax subsidy that has been referred to is more than 50 percent greater than what the federal government now spends on Medicaid. From the point of view of equity or fairness, we are spending much more on the middle and upper middle classes in a hidden way than we are publicly for the people who need it the most.

Larry Lewin made a point that I do not necessarily disagree with but I would like to question: that it is the responsibility of state legislators to find a way to pay for care for indigent patients. There are more indigent patients in the hospitals in Detroit than anywhere else in the country. Is it really Michigan's problem to finance them, is it the problem of the other hospitals or insurers in Michigan to finance them through a shift or a tax or a state pool, or is it really a broader responsibility of all members of society? I lean to the last view, certainly in that kind of example. If we broaden the problem beyond the unemployed to high-risk patients who cannot get insurance and other people who fall between the cracks, we get back to my first point, which is that this whole debate is a result of lack of revenues. If the money were there to finance those people, this debate would not be held.

I have said that the cost shift is cost sharing, and maybe in 80 percent of the cases there is nothing wrong with that shift; there is nothing wrong with the middle-class patient subsidizing the old and the poor through insurance. Maybe the shift should not be hidden; maybe it should be made more explicit through an excise tax or a tax cap. But it is wrong in examples such as Detroit, where a public hospital cannot shift to anyone because it does not have private patients, or in unique circumstances where a patient load is lopsided, which just means that the shift is not being equitably distributed.

I agree wholeheartedly that we are in an era of the purchaser, where it is everyone for himself, and this could produce a cost shift in itself. I am a firm believer in preferred provider organizations, tough negotiations, and everybody getting the best deal he can, as happens everywhere else in the marketplace. Some of the critics of this approach are going to raise the specter of denial of freedom of choice and cost shifting as a result. If a company is able to negotiate a discount with a group of providers and get a better deal and hold down its health costs, either through a self-insured plan or through a plan offered by Blue Cross or a commercial insurance company, in the short run the providers who are nonparticipating, the hospitals and doctors who cannot get the low bid, are going to raise their charges even more to make up for lost volume to the preferred provider organization. Thus one way of fighting back against the cost shift could shift costs to someone else. Since I start by agreeing that the cost shift is not inherently evil, that does not bother me, but beyond that I think in the long run it will pay off. Theoretically, nonparticipating doctors and hospitals will feel the pressure of having lost market share to those who have negotiated and will reduce their prices to get it back or retain any semblance of the marketplace, and the net result may be a reduction of costs rather than an increase. But that problem is there: it is almost like adverse selection.

When we talk about the era of the purchaser and look at good data on what providers are charging and what kind of utilization review is being done for certain types of admissions, we are led inescapably to the conclusion that if all this happens, we will also be in the age of specialization. In other words, when it comes to the hospital, a prudent purchaser cannot afford to look at aggregate data. It may very well find that, for 10 percent of the cases of its employees in one area, one hospital and one group of doctors are the correct preferred providers while for another type of case another may be. The providers also know that, which leads me to believe that we will look much more carefully at specialization than we have in the past.

The legal obstacles to preferred provider plans need to be examined carefully; legislation is pending in Congress that would try to remove some of them. About twenty-five or thirty states have removed such statutes or never had them. If we are going to be able to fight back with all the weapons we need, we must see what obstacles are in the path and get rid of them.

MR. ESCH: I am sitting here and thinking what I would do if I were representing a corporation today. I hope the panel will begin to focus on what is going to happen to the people in this audience in the next five years who have major corporate responsibility to provide adequate health care for their employees. I hope the panel will tell us what is going to happen and that government public policies are going to be predictable and are not going to hamper the private sector. Or are they? I wish someone would answer that.

COMMENT: They certainly will not be predictable.

MR. ESCH: We can predict that they will not be predictable. Dr. Kaufman represents another hospital center. We have heard from the umbrella group, but the fact that he has the term "doctor" in front of his name qualifies him as the next speaker because someone said we will never have a physician on the panel.

RONALD P. KAUFMAN, George Washington University Medical Center: In my comments I will wear a variety of hats. I have practiced internal medicine, both privately and institutionally; I now have responsibility for a 250-man group practice, an HMO, and a 500-bed hospital; and we recently signed a contract with a major insurance firm in Hartford, Connecticut, for a PPO. This action provoked a resolution of condemnation and censure from the AMA; so I decided that we are probably on the right track.

I was interested this morning that one of the new models mentioned was the PPO. Those of us who are old enough remember that Blue Shield invented PPOs some forty years ago.

On the subject of cost shifting, I will not argue whether it is good or bad, whether it exists or not, whether society wants it or not, but rather take the position that Mr. Wardrop took this morning: if we want to do something effective in this arena, we must shrink the health care system. You all know how we got this big health care system; it took forty years to get the installed capacity that we now call first-rate medical care through Hill Burton, third-party payers, titles XVIII and XIX, NIH, and health professional education legislation. Suddenly in 1980 we had a huge system. We have to shrink this system if we want to have less and ultimately at less cost; all the rest is minor tinkering.

One group we cannot shrink is the physicians. We are pumping out more and more all the time; some 18,000 U.S.-trained physicians are coming out of the pipeline every year, most of them young, and they will be around for forty or fifty years. So the option of shrinking them in numbers is not a major one.

If society agrees that it wants to shrink the system, does not want to increase taxes, and does not want to increase the percentage of GNP going into health—if it can cope with wanting everything and not wanting to pay for it and decide that we do not want artificial hearts in everybody or two or three liver transplants in all infants—we have to focus on the two things we can shrink. Those two things are hospitals and high technology, which is primarily associated with hospitals; that is where the money is.

One way to shrink them is the federal approach. It does not work very well; it results in cost shifting, and hospitals that are unable to shift costs—county hospitals, hospitals located in the ghettoes—because there is no one to shift them to will fail. Society must decide whether that is the option it is really looking for.

Another approach to cutting down on total capacity would be national health insurance on the egalitarian model of one standard for all and a mechanism to keep the technology and the access down. We have heard a lot today about the free market approach but suggest that the free market may not act out society's desire. Those who can pay will, those who are big enough to negotiate will, those who cannot do that will not have that opportunity, and we may end up decreasing the size, but not in a selective manner.

I suggest a different approach; that is, that health care delivery is a local phenomenon that must be packaged for local consumption and local issues. If we want to size down in a fair manner, we have to do something not dissimilar to what we do with fire departments and the public school system: let local areas determine how many stationhouses and fire engines or how many grade schools and high schools they want to pay for and then allocate the resources necessary to support that capacity. This can be done by a governmental agency, through a coalition, or through some other organization. That would be the major way to cut down the capacity and ration in a rational manner, not in a haphazard manner as we are now doing.

MR. ESCH: Stan Jones represents a major research group, and he has also had experience in Blue Cross–Blue Shield and on the Hill.

STANLEY B. JONES, Health Policy Alternatives Incorporated: I suggest that the notion of cost shifting really glosses over three questions that are much more important than the cost-shifting debate gives credence to.

The first question is, What costs of hospitals do we want to pay? If we would like to shrink the health care system, then asking what costs we want to pay is a very tough question. Have in mind that we do not want to pay as much as we have been paying. At least we do not want the system to grow as fast as it has been growing, and perhaps it even ought to shrink. If there are operating margins or profit margins that seem to be the makings of growth, what costs we want to pay is the first and most important question.

The second question is, Who should pay those costs? One easy answer is that they should be spread equally over all payers;.but when we start looking at the situation closely, we find that the government payer may not be responsible for quite as much of those things as others but perhaps should pick up more research costs or things of that sort. It is a complicated question.

The third and maybe most insidious question is, Who should decide the answers to the first two questions and on what basis? I have heard two extreme answers suggested at this table, and I think most people here are in between.

One answer, for example, is to say the states should decide what costs should be paid and should allocate them among payers by some criterion. The criterion frequently used in the debate is equity among payers. That is one I have always had trouble with. I have been in the health policy business a long time, and I have gotten excited about access and about equity in the sense of seeing that lower-income people get a fair share, but equity among insurers has always left me cold. There has to be a better criterion than that. But, again, who decides, and by what criterion?

Another and equally radical answer is that the buyer decides. If the buyer is an HMO, it decides what it wants to buy from a hospital and how much it wants to pay, and that is what it pays for, and the constraint on it is the marketplace. If there are people who want to buy that product on that basis, competing with other products, then it is a credible product. Likewise an insurer ought to make whatever deal it can get as long as the subscriber wants to continue to sign up for the package the insurer negotiates with the hospital. Somewhere between those two extremes I think our future lies. We could talk about all the options without using the term *cost shifting,* and we would probably be better off for doing so.

The underlying question is, How fast do we want the health care system to grow? Or do we want it to shrink? If that is what we want, what is the best way to get it? Should we let government shrink the system? Should we let 100 or 200 or 1,000 payers work to shrink it by the deals they strike? That is the real set of questions.

MR. ESCH: We have some representatives here from the White House, the Department of Health and Human Services, and the Hill. Let us start with Glenn Hackbarth.

GLENN HACKBARTH, Department of Health and Human Services: Stan Jones posed a nice set of questions. I wish I had concrete answers. I can make a few general observations, the most important being that the administration's position is that we ought to minimize the extent to which government is responsible for making centralized choices on these difficult questions. There are many reasons for that, but they fall into two general categories, one philosophical and the other pragmatic.

The philosophical reason is that we think there are reasonable, legitimate differences of opinion about what constitutes adequate medical care in particular cases and for particular groups, and there is no single right style of care that we would feel comfortable in mandating for all segments of the population. We cannot say that a certain number of CAT scanners is the right number for a particular group to have or that there is a right number of hospital beds. Those questions are all very subjective, and we would like to see as decentralized a decision-making process as possible.

The more pragmatic reason for opposing centralization, at least at the federal level, is that the government is not up to the task. Many people have lamented the irrationality of the government reimbursement policy and of government decision making on a number of health care financing issues, including coverage as well as reimbursement. I wonder where the wisdom is to come from that will guide us to the right answers to these very complicated questions. It seems to me that given the highly politicized environment in which I do my work and people on the Hill do their work, the system is irrational. We work in a political system that has many good traits, but it does not always lend itself to careful, pragmatic decision making. The critics of the cost shift would probably be the first to recognize that, if there is a cost shift and it is an important economic force, it is the byproduct of a very complicated political environment.

All that said, I recognize that the other polar extreme—of relying on the private sector in thousands of negotiations to sort out these questions—is a very messy solution if it is a solution at all. Certainly there are going to be inequities in this system, and ten years from now there will be similar groups sitting in similar rooms talking about these issues. But my final judgment is that we have to tolerate that messiness, that we have to take on small problems and resolve the problems piecemeal. It just isn't feasible or ultimately desirable to vest in the federal government the authority to say what is the right amount of resources and what is the fair share for that payer or for that other payer.

WILLIAM L. ROPER, Office of Policy Development: I have been in Washington since September, working as a White House fellow on the domestic policy staff, and I could hardly have picked a more exciting, frustrating, challenging time to be involved in health policy. I had hoped that the process would work its way through one cycle in the year that I have been here, but Congress has not been quite so accommodating and has not acted with great dispatch on all parts of the president's health care cost containment package.

The president has spoken very eloquently in his message to the Congress of February 28, 1983, along with the package of bills that went forward to the Congress asking for changes in the incentives in our health care system. The term "health care incentives reform proposal" was a carefully chosen title, implying (1) that what the president and his cabinet would like to see is a change in incentives to bring price and negotiation about price and competition more into play; and (2) that the proper role of government is to get out of the way and let normal market forces take hold and try to check the escalating health care costs. Congress acted very quickly on the prospective payment for Medicare. The rest of the program is still before Congress, and if it is not acted on this time, there will be another round in years to come. But there are some things coming due that we cannot forever postpone action on, some fundamental actions that need to be taken.

I have had a chance recently to think about some very basic misperceptions about our health care system; there are some myths abroad about that system. The first is that inflation is the only problem, the health care cost inflation. You have heard about how the medical component of the consumer price index in the early months of 1983 was three times the CPI, but that is a temporary phenomenon. The real cause of the massive driving up of expenditures in health care is that we are using the system far more than we did ten, twenty, or thirty years ago.

A second myth is that we can find some scapegoat—greedy doctors or ripoff hospitals or the poor or the elderly—and say they are causing this problem.They are not really; it is all of us. We all have wanted more than we have been willing to pay for, as Jack Meyer has told us today.

Another myth that clouds the debate is that it is beyond individual patients to deal with the problem, that government or somebody has to help them with it, that they cannot make decisions based on price, that they are not sufficiently well informed to make those kinds of decisions. Certainly they ought to be better informed than they are, but if economics has taught us anything, it is that people will respond to incentives—that when they have a stake in the matter, they will buy things that are less expensive. The president's program is directed to giving people the opportunity to make those choices.

Another myth is that if we try to improve the productivity of the health care system, its quality inevitably will suffer, and the specter is always invoked that we have a wonderful health care system that will be destroyed. That is not the case; those of you who are involved in the system know where productivity gains can be made that will allow lower prices to be charged. But the opposite side of that is that productivity gains are not limitless; finally we will come up against the fact that we cannot continue to spend stupendously large amounts on health care of the very ill if we are to come to grips with health care costs. The very ill tend to be the very young and the very old, and that arouses all sorts of emotions. But if we are going to grapple with that problem, I am not willing to let government be the one grappling with it. I think individuals have to have a stake in the matter.

Of all the myths about the health care system, the most pernicious is that nothing can be done, that there is no solution, that somehow these problems are beyond us and we ought to give up, be satisfied with the status quo. Congress's quick action on prospective payment tells us that is not the case; all around us people in the private sector are saying that they are not satisfied with the status quo and, whatever government does, they will cause change in the health care system. That is a hopeful sign whatever happens. Whether or not government makes any changes at all, there will be changes, and when we come back in five years, the health care system will be radically different from the one that we see now.

ROBERT E. PATRICELLI, CIGNA Corporation: I will just make three points. First, Bernie Tresnowski was mostly wrong, and Mike Bromberg was mostly right. That may surprise them both, but I think I heard Bernie Tresnowski say that cost shifting was all right because it was really the product of freely negotiated arm's-length transactions between the payers and the providers. Of course, if that were the case, he would be mostly right, but it is not. I do not believe that government cost shifting is a result of government's arriving at the prices it will pay through open market negotiation with providers. Nor is it possible for payers in the private sector other than Blue Cross and Blue Shield to aggregate their purchasing power sufficiently to be able to negotiate in the same way the Blues have. For many years the commercial insurers have been seeking a limited antitrust exemption to permit them to do that and have been unable to get it. So there are some problems with cost shifting because it is not a matter of freely negotiated outcomes. Mike Bromberg is right: we have to fix it not because it is ethically wrong, not because the political process could not decide to have a hidden subsidy, but because it is undermining proper incentives and is obstructing solutions to our problems. You do not have to like commercial insurers versus the Blues or a very big corporation versus others to be against cost shifting. You do not have to take a position on grounds of ethics or fairness. Cost shifting is getting in the way because, without some equity in the payment system, employers are finding their own cost-containing incentives undercut. If they have to bear increasing burdens on behalf of other patients than their own, their ability to see results from their own cost-containing efforts is undercut. Hospitals do not have the same incentives to contain costs when the cost-shifting opportunity is open to them. Equity is needed to avoid an even more serious development of a two-class system of care in this country, which we are moving toward.

The statement was made this morning by Bill Goldbeck that he was worried about access. We should all worry about access because cost shifting is going to get us back to the search for lower-cost providers, which means providers who deal less often with government-paid patients. We are going to find in the preferred provider movement an effort by insurers and buyers and other purchasers of care to identify those who can provide care for less money, and that means those providers who do not have to bear cost shifts. If we do not deal with the cost shift problem, we are going to drift toward a two-class system. I would say further that equity is necessary to stimulate competition and privatization in the system. Like Jack Meyer, I am a believer in establishing a Medicare voucher, but I also believe we can't get there from here because of the cost shift obstruction. Those of us in the insurance industry cannot play in that game with a 20 percent differential, and it would be wise for the government to try to privatize the Medicare program in some fashion, but cost shifts are in the way. So let's fix it because it is a problem, not because of an ethical concern.

Finally, what should the public sector do about it? Here is where I come back to Mike Bromberg, and I think it has to pay up. It is as simple as that. We can argue about which form of taxation is the most efficient. I am glad to hear people talking about the tax cap approach as a method of revenue raising rather than as a cost-containing device, which I do not believe it ever was. We can have reasonable disagreements about whether it is a good revenue-raising approach. But the government ought to pay up; exactly how much it ought to pay I don't know, but whatever it is paying now is not fair and is not enough. Second, even if the government were in some fashion paying its fair share, there would still obviously be problems with health cost escalation. We have made one proposal that deals with Jack Meyer's criticism of an all-payer prospective payment system. There is a tendency to say that anybody who is for all-payer systems must want rate regulation across the board. That is not necessarily the case, and it is not our proposal. The approach I suggest is that government make it possible for all payers to buy prospectively, but not set the prices. Simply put, our proposal would be that the government require hospitals by some future date to post prices for private payers by DRG category and permit insurers and private payers to buy at those prices or to continue to pay on a fee-for-service basis if they choose. These would not be the same prices Medicare is paying, but simply posted prices so that the hospitals are at risk and we can buy prospectively. That would, we believe, set in train competitive juices without involving government in rate setting across the board.

PAUL GINSBURG, Congressional Budget Office: I am paying a price for being the last speaker. I thought I had some interesting things to say when I came; then I heard the other speakers say them very eloquently. Let me take a couple of minutes to repeat them with a little different emphasis.

I see cost shifting as a symptom of our inaction in the public policy sphere with respect to the major decisions in the allocation of health care resources. When there is a difference in price between what some payers are paying and what hospital charges are, it has two major sources. One is the financing of care for the indigent, those not covered by Medicare and Medicaid, and the other what some payers would consider prudent purchasing on their behalf, using their market power not to pay more than they think is an appropriate price. These two sources reflect decisions that need to be made but have not been.

On indigent care, we seem to have two different messages. The federal government in 1965 and again in 1972 made some very explicit decisions about whom it was willing to pay for in the Medicare and Medicaid programs and thus whom it was not willing to pay for. The issue that we need to confront is the rest of the low-income people, who were not singled out by these programs. Are they to get good access to health care or not? There seems to be a consensus that they should be getting good access to health care. In debates—say between those in Mike Bromberg's industry and those in the not-for-profit industry—Mike Bromberg's people often say, "We do as much charity care as you do, and we are doing what a good hospital is supposed to do." So I wonder if we have a value out there. The hospitals ought to provide good care for the indigent, but the public has explicitly decided that it is not going to pay. We need to resolve what kind of care the indigent should have and who is going to pay for it.

The next decision that we have not made is how we are going to contain health care costs—and there seems to be a growing consensus about that. When we cut through all the rhetoric, there are only two ways we can contain health care costs. One is through market forces; this can be through standard things like cost sharing, newfangled names for it like preferred provider organizations—which are very similar to the old-fashioned indemnity policies that passed out of popularity many years ago—through capitation, or through health maintenance organizations. Anyway, market forces are one way. Regulation is the other. If we embarked on either one, we would not have a cost-shifting problem. Consider the prudent purchaser actions the federal government has taken with Medicare, paying on a DRG basis. In a sense government has made the decision that it wants to use its centralized buying power to influence hospital costs rather than the decentralized power of the Medicare beneficiaries by restructuring benefits or cost sharing. But because the rest of the system has neither market forces nor regulation, the hospitals can shift the reimbursement reductions to other payers. Clearly, if we had regulation for the other payers or market forces—meaning that the other purchasers of care were very sensitive to the prices charged—then hospitals would not have the option of shifting costs. They would have no recourse but to reduce their costs or to take losses on their operating statements.

Cost shifting reflects decisions not made; it could very well get worse in the process of making those decisions when we make them one step at a time. I see no solutions to cost shifting per se except as part of broader solutions to these basic health care issues.

DR. WILSON: I would like to recommend a book by Paul Starr, a Harvard sociologist, *The Social Transformation of American Medicine*. It follows the transformation of medicine from the alms house to the present time.

I mentioned some schizophrenia among physicians, and there is a schizophrenia about physicians as well; I want to put that thought in your head. Are physicians to be members of an honored profession and practice as such, or are we to act like businessmen? What does the public wish us to do? It seems to me this whole debate is heading toward a great war between Massachusetts and California. Massachusetts is seen to be clinging to one standard of care, and that may be the way the pendulum swings, while California has a chopped-liver approach with many tiers, not just two tiers, of care. Is that what you want from medicine as a commodity?

Second, if the federal government has its way, it will establish DRGs for payment of physicians; if this system spills over into the private sector, it is certainly rate setting.

Another point I wish to raise is that I think it is wrong for the government to say that it cannot set a standard or style of care for what it purchases. Certainly medicine can be practiced in different ways, but it is time that we did set a standard of care for governments that buy care for the poor. We have to talk about those nitty-gritty philosophical and ethical issues of liver transplants and artificial hearts: how many do they benefit, and at what cost? The government must take a look at where the National Institutes of Health put their money. Who benefits? If society pays, society should benefit. There are some perversions in all parts of the system—we haven't touched on that.

MR. ESCH: What's going on in the arena of local initiatives and the relations between the public and the private sectors? I will ask Rosemary Gibson to give us an overview of that.

ROSEMARY GIBSON, American Enterprise Institute: We have discussed the public-private sector relationship in rather negative terms, that is, in terms of cost shift—the public sector is a headache for the private sector. AEI has been undertaking a series of site visits and discussions with state Medicaid directors and budget officials, taking a look at how they are making changes in their Medicaid programs, essentially paralleling the activities that you in the business sector are undertaking. How can we change the incentives through which we provide and finance medical service, in this case not for your employees but for the indigent? One of the crucial factors in the success of some of these initiatives is the extent to which there is a vibrant health care market, with payers becoming purchasers and providers becoming sellers of services. I would hypothesize that the extent to which some of the state initiatives to bring incentives into public programs can be successful is contingent on the extent to which there is an active private market.

Let me explain all this in reference to one particular state. The state has received a waiver from the Department of Health and Human Services to establish a relatively new model of health care delivery and financing, what we call a primary care network or case management. Essentially that does three things. First, it changes the incentives for states. States in some instances receive capitation payments now instead of open-ended matching payments from the federal government. Second, it changes incentives for providers, puts them at relative degrees of risk whereas now they are paid on a fee-for-service basis. Third, it changes the incentives for patients and holds down the abuse and the use of unauthorized services in the health care system.

These changing incentives in the public sector parallel the kinds of things that businesses such as the ones represented here today are attempting. My prognosis is that the state activities may not gain a foothold, because Medicaid is not, at least in this particular state, a major payer of hospital services and the few relatively large private payers in the system are not actively turning from payers into purchasers of medical services. Hence the incentives for providers are not really changing; providers still operating on a fee-for-service basis are reluctant to change to a prepaid system. With this private and public sector relationship, it is crucial that the private sector can set the framework and provide an impetus for states to undertake the kinds of activities that you are doing in the private sector.

In response to the point about the need for shrinking the system, I do not see why there cannot be shrinkage of the supply of physicians. We have an example of shrinkage on the panel: Bill Roper is not a practicing physician, he is here in the policy arena. I suggest that as the market becomes increasingly competitive, physicians may choose other careers.

MR. ESCH: The work that you are doing on the public-private relationship is especially significant because so many people in this room, although they are in the private sector and trying to shape it, are really saying that they should not be afraid to begin to shape the public sector too.

MR. TRESNOWSKI: Bob Patricelli mentioned the need for market leverage to negotiate. Bill Guy, popularly known as the Medi-Cal czar, has negotiated for the past year for the Medi-Cal program. I asked him why he got involved, and he said he had learned an important lesson when he was the head of the Blue Cross plan in Southern California. After negotiating with a hospital in Los Angeles for fifteen years, he was able to obtain a 1 percent differential. Along came an HMO that promised patient flow of about 3 percent and extracted a 20 percent differential. The lesson he learned is that channeling is what is important, not the amount of market leverage. I think that is what has given rise to what has gone on in California and indeed what is behind the new emphasis on preferred provider organizations.

On the matter of Medicare not being a negotiating environment, a lot of negotiation takes place in the drafting of legislation. In 1965, 1966, and 1967 the American Hospital Association negotiated a 2 percent override, which helped the net margins of institutions substantially over a period of fifteen years. I agree on the point about cost shifting getting in the way because I agree with Stan Jones and Paul Ginsburg that it is a symptom of more fundamental problems that need to be addressed: how we are going to take care of poor people who cannot afford care and how we are going to contain health care costs.

MR. ESCH: In the political arena, we have tried to avoid the question of how we are going to take care of the indigent, and we have developed elaborate schemes for you in the private sector or you in the public sector to try to say, "If we hide it enough, it will go away," rather than admitting it up front.

DR. MEYER: I would say that the federal deficits are the aggregation of doing that in all sectors, not just health care.

MR. ESCH: Then the price we are paying is for not admitting that we can be a large but benevolent government that is efficiently and effectively run.

CONSTANCE BERNTON, Trinity College: I would like to comment briefly on something that Dr. Meyer said and that many of you have referred to in passing. A number of years ago there was full funding for dialysis care in kidney disease, and anyone who had that disease could get remarkable amounts of funds. Someone else mentioned that we have cut the budget for prenatal care for mothers who are dependent on public financing and that we may be getting low-weight babies, which require a lot of money for special care. I think the time has come when we have to say what we want to spend our health care dollars for. Nobody wants to make that value judgment, but when we have insufficient funds, we have to begin addressing these issues.

MR. ESCH: Do we make those decisions on a monolithic basis? How do we handle those decisions within the system?

COMMENT: This may be reiterating a point I made earlier, but we tend to talk about government as though it were a separate entity unrelated to those of us who pay the taxes. If we look at the leverage that a dollar invested in prevention of a severely retarded child or of simply an unpaid bill means to us as corporate taxpayers, it is obvious that we must try to persuade state governments to put the available dollars, including even more dollars of our taxes, to work in these leveraged ways. It makes a lot of sense for corporations to spend a little extra money to get coverage for these populations because they end up paying less in the cost that gets shifted to them if those investments are not made. So I think the point is well taken; the numbers of high-risk infants are going up, infant mortality and morbidity are growing, and we end up paying very high prices for these consequences.

ETHEL STEVENS, Union County Medical Society of New Jersey: I come from the DRG state of New Jersey. I am disappointed that none of you chose to have someone here to talk about the wonderful system that we have. New Jersey is one of the most highly regulated states in the nation. We have DRGs; we have a new pilot program of Medicaid capitation; we have rate setting. We have a commissioner of health who decided to limit the number of CAT scanners we had. That didn't work, and we now have a commissioner of health who is going to limit how many beds we have, and that's not going to work either. None of the systems they impose on us seem to work very well.

Working as I do as a director for an 850-member medical society of physicians, I sit there in New Jersey and ponder all these questions, and it is scary to come down here and face the best brains in the business and find they don't have any answers either because we certainly don't have them up there.

There is one thing you have overlooked, and that is that your best resource is your doctor. That doctor is giving a lot of care, and he is giving a lot of it free to these indigents you talk about.

Just for a moment I want to talk about cost shifting because I want to talk about my lady. My lady called me just the other day (I get a lot of calls from the public so that I do a sort of counseling). She is a fifty-four-year-old lady who was a patient at one of our hospitals. She had insurance from a company that paid 100 percent of charges, but of course we have DRGs. She was nine days in the hospital, and the DRG bill was $7,000. Her insurance company paid 100 percent of charges, which came to $3,080. That lady wasn't indigent before, but now she has a $4,000 hospital bill to pay, and she surely is going to be indigent very soon because she's not a well lady. Her insurance company got the best deal it could, and the government got the best deal it could. Only one person cannot shift that cost, and that is that lady.

MR. ESCH: We must have a system that is in total support of the professionals who have the ability to relate to the patient and perform professionally in a competent manner. That is what the whole health care system is about. Sometimes we get so involved with systems and policy that we fail to keep that focus, that ultimately the health care has to be provided for the patient by the professional.

DR. MEYER: I would like to respond briefly to the previous comment because I occasionally do a radio talk show and your lady is always on the other end of the call-in and I never have a good answer for her. There are so many folks fifty-four years old or thereabouts who fall between the cracks of the kinds of private sector protection that mainstream Americans have through the workplace and public sector programs. That has gotten worse in recent years because we have drawn the safety net even tighter around a certain group, which we call categorically eligible for aid, a certain kind of poor people, and more and more people are out in the cold.

We do not need to think in terms of national health insurance, but whom are we going to help if we raise two billion through the tax subsidy cap? Whom are we going to give it to, the unemployed automobile worker or that lady? There are some fundamental equity issues that we have to address here. It seems to me that one can simultaneously be concerned about the heavy hand of the federal government as a regulator of the health care system and still be concerned about that lady. One of the attractions of certain market-oriented proposals to me, such as the one introduced by Congressman Richard Gephardt of Missouri, is that they express both a concern with the heavy presence of the federal government in the system and a concern for those who fall between the cracks. We need to give a little more attention to both problems than we have.

MR. HAVIGHURST: I was going to ask Bob Patricelli to explain to me once again—I have heard the explanation for ten years, but I still don't understand it—why the commercial insurers don't have enough bargaining power to drive a hard bargain. Bernie Tresnowski's comment struck me as so telling, as going right to the heart of the matter, as devastating, and nobody seemed to appreciate that; so I smelled blood, and I thought I ought to move in for the kill.

COMMENT: This is Havighurst playing *agent provocateur*.

MR. HAVIGHURST: The point really is, Isn't your lack of bargaining power traceable to your lack of ability to move your patients from place to place? Obviously you can ask the hospital to give you a lower price, and they might even do it; but they have no reason to do it because they have nothing to gain—you have nothing to take away from them as long as you cannot control where your patients go. Many people in this audience represent employers. They are concerned about how to control costs, and they need to appreciate the great importance of the ability to move patients, to direct the patient flow to providers who are giving a better price or a better service, better value for the money. The commercial insurers' great failure has always been that they have no capacity, and no interest in developing a capacity, to serve their customers, the employers, in this manner. Why isn't that the heart of the problem? Why would an antitrust exemption help you if you still don't have that ability?

MR. PATRICELLI: You are ascribing some motives that I will take more issue with than some of the other things you said. Let me start by saying that things are changing. What would not have been possible five years ago with hospitals may be possible now. Commercial insurers and their employer customers are talking very actively about trying to engage in these kinds of discussions with providers. Indeed, that is what PPOs are all about, but until we began to see some of the concern by hospitals and physicians that we are now seeing, a concern for market share, hospitals simply were not going to be moved when individual insurers like CIGNA, which might represent at best a few hundred certificate holders in a metropolitan area, tried to negotiate a price break. We were willing enough to do it, as shown by our desire over the years to get concerted buying power by acting together. That is where I take exception to your comment about our not being interested. We were certainly interested and had become convinced that we could only do it collectively, given the providers' resistance. Now the patterns are changing. There are some other people in the industry in the audience who may want to have a run at the question.

MR. ESCH: I would like to hear Bernie Tresnowski, of Blue Cross–Blue Shield, on that, because certainly you represent a larger population than one individual insurer. What do you do to leverage?

MR. TRESNOWSKI: I think Bob Patricelli is quite correct that things are changing. St. Paul and Minneapolis have been in the forefront of HMO development. HMOs constitute about 40 percent of the market share there. Blue Cross–Blue Shield had a dwindling share of the market, and so they had to do something. What they did was to come up with a preferred provider product, which they call AWARE. They negotiated a price with seventeen of the twenty-six hospitals in the Twin Cities area and went into the market with that. I recently read the literature the plan has distributed, which said to the subscriber, "Here is a product. You can receive comprehensive benefits for care in an AWARE hospital. If your doctor is not an AWARE doctor, get yourself a new doctor."

MR. BROMBERG: I just want to add a little bit. I think Clark Havighurst was gracious. There were other things he could have added, like utilization review and getting tough on outliers, not just pricing. I don't think it is all that new; other people have done it first, and commercial insurers are just seeing the light. The occupancy rate in California has been in the 60 percent range for ten years, but this is one example where innovations in the private sector have occurred first. The real problem has been that the system did not give you the economic incentive to do it; the tax subsidy has been such that you would have been foolish to do it. It is not just you; it is us too. The system has been such for years that we would have been stupid to be better managers. We would have taken the money out of our own pocket by being too efficient because we were under cost reimbursement. The system has said something very similar to you. Now the system is starting to change for us, and we will see over the next few years how we respond to it, but it still has not changed with regard to the commercials except insofar as you are feeling some loss of market share from self-insurance and you are feeling some innovative things being done by business. If one company in one city can do it, how can a big commercial insurance company not do it?

MR. PATRICELLI: It is true that until recently it was not in commercial insurers' business and marketing makeup to go hard into these kinds of things because the employers were not concerned about them. They were concerned about the prompt and efficient payment of claims. Commercial insurers probably represented them pretty well in that regard. Now the world has changed for all of us. The most important marketing consideration now for commercial insurers is how good they are on cost containment; so we are out there scrapping and fighting with everybody else to come up with the best data systems, the best PPOs, and all the rest. The whole world has changed very rapidly in the last five years, and we are going to move along as quickly as we can.

MR. LEWIN: The last point Bob Patricelli made is the one I wanted to make. Neither the Blue Cross plans nor the private insurance companies were being really aggressive at the kinds of things we are seeing now. If we look at how employers were making decisions not only among private insurers but between Blue Cross and insurers, we see a whole different ballgame from what it is today. That employers have taken so long to wake up to this is an interesting phenomenon, only part of which is explained by the tax cap. It probably had more to do with not wanting to take on the unions or invite unions by tinkering with a very sensitive area of benefits. But it is now at the point where the issue that was management prerogatives and work rules of the 1940s and 1950s has become health benefits in the 1980s.

MR. HAVIGHURST: Bob Patricelli's remarks are very reassuring to me; I asked the question to prompt that kind of response. But if it is true that the commercial insurers are now in a position where they can bargain and are willing to do so, why are they so resistant to and concerned about the tax cap and so supportive of regulation and all-payer systems? Why do we have the Blues opposed to all-payer systems and the commercials so in favor of them? If the commercials are really able and willing to bargain hard, presumably they can protect themselves against the cost shift. That seems to me to be the way things ought to head, and I am still troubled by the extent to which the commercials are leading the fight for regulation.

MR. ARNOULD: I want to talk now, not as a professor but as a hospital trustee, on bargaining power. I know that if our hospital is running around 79 to 82 percent occupancy or higher, we are doing very well. We can think about new programs, we can think about expansion—not necessarily capital facilities, but a program. When we go much below that, particularly around 75 percent occupancy or lower, we are talking about the survival of existing programs or even about cutting programs. That is not much of a range. So you do not have to be very large to catch our attention. We do not have to lose too many patients or too many groups before we start to listen to you. We are not necessarily going to go into full-scale discounting, but we are going to do things to keep your employees in our hospital. You have a lot of power even if you are not an enormous insurance company.

DR. KAUFMAN: I think the point that Bob Patricelli made earlier should be emphasized again: if the insurance company does not have the ability to shift the patient, they have no negotiating power with the provider. In other words, if you do not control the doctors and where they are going to admit the patient, you can negotiate until you are blue in the face, but you will not get a price because you cannot influence the market share. If you want to get into that realm, you have to go into HMOs and PPOs, where you can control providers and dictate to the consumers where they are going to get care under that policy, a situation nobody was interested in until about four or five years ago.

COMMENT: Has it been the public policy that has discouraged that patient mobility, and is it shifting now?

COMMENT: I think it was a number of different policies. It was the tax issue; it was employers who were not much interested in what percentage health costs were of the product they were making; it was that nobody really cared. They wanted to buy the Cadillac for every patient who came in, and the world has changed.

MR. ESCH: I will now turn to Larry Lewin for an overview.

MR. LEWIN: I feel a little bit like punting here because this panel has managed to focus on issues in a way that almost makes a summary redundant. We have had disagreements, but we have had rather sharp convergence on some issues—for example, that there is an option for purchasers and through them their insurers to deal with cost shifting as a prudent purchaser phenomenon in a way that can put the pressure back on providers effectively. The point we have just been arguing has been a very good one.

Perhaps we have not dealt as extensively as we might with the subject of indigent care. Mike Bromberg's point that the federal government, not state governments, might very well be the focus of concern in answering the questions who should be covered and who should pay, is an important one.

Maybe the most important point raised here this afternoon was Stan Jones's third question: now that we know what the questions are, to whom are we going to look to answer them? That will probably be the most troubling, not only because of the federal-state split but simply because the questions themselves are difficult and we are not well armed to deal with ethical concerns.

Although many of these questions may seem lofty or philosophical, I believe they are all worthy of the attention and action of each individual employer, whether that action be through communication with employees to try to get them to understand the issues better or through membership on boards of trustees of institutions or through negotiations with provider groups or through dealings with state legislatures or collectively through associations—either local coalitions or trade associations—with elected officials. All these issues lend themselves to your influence. I thought Bob Patricelli's point was a telling one: that commercial insurers, like Blue Cross, might have been able to do more but there has been very little reason for them to do it because you were not demanding it. Times have changed, but whether they change as dramatically as they could depends on how aggressively those of us who are paying the bills take responsibility for the cost.

MR. ESCH: How do you provide for equitable coverage with limited resources in a diversified structure, and what part does your corporation play in those decisions? When I went to Hungary, I learned from one of the State Department people that they had to supply their maid with two cartons of American cigarettes when she went into the major hospital in Hungary to deliver because the only way to get a single bed was to offer American cigarettes. So much for centralized health care systems. I will ask Jack Meyer to summarize for us.

DR. MEYER: It is very difficult to summarize. We have had different opinions regarding the questions that Stan Jones raised and different roles outlined for the federal government, state governments, and the private sector. We have differentiated the kinds of roles the government might take as the subsidizer of the indigent. One question that comes up again and again is, Who will cover the indigent people who are not in these programs? This comes up in health care and also in other sectors of our social structure. The debate is over the plausibility and feasibility of new approaches to this problem that involve more direct, explicit subsidies instead of the old way that we are used to, which is a very indirect way, a kind of hidden tax. There are advantages and disadvantages of each for fairness and efficiency. I thank all the panelists for being candid. That has made for a good day, and I think we have all enjoyed it.